ALWAYS A PILGRIM

Walking the Zen Christian Path

Thomas G. Hand, S.J.

Mercy Center Meditation Program
2300 Adeline Drive • Burlingame, CA 94010

Always A Pilgrim
is published by Mercy Center Meditation Program

For information contact:
Mercy Center Meditation Program
2300 Adeline Drive
Burlingame, CA 94010

Illustrations by
Su Ja Kim

Printed by
The General Printing Company
Berkeley, California
www.generalprint.com

ISBN 0-88739-621-6
Library of Congress Catalog Number 2004115680

Printed in the United States of America

To all the Mercy Center Meditators
for years of companionship
on The Way

Burlingame, CA
2004

ACKNOWLEDGEMENTS

It is impossible for me to mention all the wonderful people who have contributed to the publication of this work. Special thanks, though, must be given to Sue Blumenberg, Kathleen Barber and Meg Marnell whose efforts in recent months brought the production to fruition. I want to thank Su Ja Kim for the beautiful brush paintings that can be found throughout the book. To these and to so many who are not named I offer my heartfelt gratitude.

CONTENTS

PART TWO: COMING BACK

INTRODUCTION

In the first year of the new millennium, I celebrated my eightieth birthday. I still look to the future and have many projects yet to actualize, God willing. This very book, although it does look back to the past, is mainly concerned with the future. It has been written as a possible help to people of any and all spiritual traditions as we walk forward together in this new century. It is a pilgrim's tale, the story of how my humanity and Christianity have been revitalized by deep and sincere contact with the East.

Pilgrims All

What is a pilgrim? The original Latin word is peregrinus, made up of per and ager. Ager is a field, as in agriculture. Per, usually "through," here has the extended meaning of "beyond" or "outside." A field, of course, includes one's place, family, culture, relationships, values, structures of thought…one's whole little world. So a pilgrim is a person who goes beyond the confines of her or his little field into a new and broader way of life.

The word "field" is felicitous and meaningful here. True human pilgrims leave the structures of their narrow, individual energy form fields, accept the more powerful energy of the great archetypal form fields, and are transformed into larger and revitalized human persons. A pilgrimage, then, is a rite of passage. You leave home, journey toward a new field, enter the shrine of the new energy, are transformed, and rise to a new and higher way of life. This is the pattern of the pilgrim, whether it be Abraham on his way to the Promised Land, a Muslim on hadji to Mecca, a Buddhist traveling to Bodhgaya, or a Christian following the paths of Jesus in the Holy Land. It is the very pattern Jesus of Nazareth fulfilled on his way to resurrection.

The Path of Knowledge

A particular characteristic of my life journey is that it has been quite intellectual. My pilgrim search has always been to know. Both of the meanings of "to know" are intended here: knowing by direct experience, and intellectual understanding of the experience. Some of the intellectual expressions of reality that I write about in this book will sound new to many people. I am well aware that to offer changes in our mental structures, especially when connected with matters of belief, is a very sensitive endeavor. However, I present these ideas not as fundamentally new doctrine but simply as new expressions of the fundamental teaching of Christ.

In his address at the opening of Vatican Council II, Pope John XXIII said, "The deposit of faith is one thing; the way that it is presented is another. For the truths preserved in our sacred doctrine can retain the same substance and meaning under different forms of expression."[1] The Council itself, in the decree on Ecumenism, says, "While preserving unity in essentials, let all members of the Church, according to the office entrusted to each, preserve a proper freedom in the various forms of spiritual life and discipline, in the variety of liturgical rites, and even in the theological elaborations of revealed truth."[2] Accepting that "freedom" as to "theological elaborations," I offer these chapters. In no way are they to be considered definitive, but simply as a sincere updating of the Christian—even the human—message. After presenting them to hundreds of people, I know that they have helped many to renew their human and Christian commitments.

Consider this book as a possible example of the development spoken of in the Vatican II Council decree on Revelation: "This tradition which comes from the apostles develops in the Church with the help of the Holy Spirit. For there is growth in the understanding of the realities and the words that have been handed down. This happens through the contemplation and study made by believers, who treasure these things in their hearts (cf. Lk. 2:19,51), through the intimate understanding of spiritual things they experience..."[3]

These words truly describe my experience, because I really do treasure in my heart the realities and words of Christ and am sincerely trying to give them a growth of understanding suited to our times. The words of Tagore beautifully describe, I would say, the needs of humanity in our times:

When old words die out on the tongue,
New melodies spring forth from the heart.[4]

"Hando"

A true name is a vocalization of the special energy form field of a given individual. As such, it is a powerful and precious thing. We should even use it as a personal, individualized mantra. When we pronounce it, it becomes a kind of invocation of that special power. This is what is at the root of Christians chanting the name of Jesus or Buddhists that of Amida Buddha. In many cultures, a new name is taken on when there is a major shift in the flow of a person's life energy. I feel that this happened to me one evening in the dining room of a small convent in Kyoto. I had stopped in to visit the Sisters of St. Joseph of Carondelet. The group sitting at the table was made up of six young Japanese women, all postulants seeking to enter the Carondelet community.

I asked them to put my name, Hand, into Sino-Japanese ideograms. They understood that I wanted something to express the developing direction of my life. Hand is pronounced "Hando" in Japanese. (Han rhymes with con. A short o is added to the d because no consonant other than n can end a Japanese word.) Hando, then, is two syllables and requires two ideograms. I don't remember exactly how it came about or who was the creator, but I was given the name . 伴渡.

The first ideogram means "to accompany"; the second, "to cross over." So I am a person who accompanies others in crossing over to the other shore—to the state of light, truth, and new life. This book has been written with the hope that in reading it you will walk the pilgrim path together with Hando. My sincere desire is that the book will be a boat in which we both cast off from our confining boundaries and cross over—not just to a better understanding, but to a new and richer reality. This is our work, until each of us individually and all of us as one have spiraled up to a higher shore of Life. We are always pilgrims...together.

A word about the poems heading each chapter of this book: They are intended to be a cameo of the chapter. Although they are written in haiku form, they are not presented as true haiku. A haiku is direct experience directly expressed; these poems are more like reflections. They follow the formula: 2-3-2+alpha. This means there are two accented syllables in the first and third lines, three accents in the second line, and any number ("alpha") of unaccented syllables distributed in any way throughout the three lines. This the English form that best expresses the 5-7-5 syllable pattern of Japanese haiku.

Note: Japanese nouns do not have different forms for singular and plural; the number is determined by context. I will follow that convention here, and not add an s to the plural of Japanese words, except for a few that have entered common English usage.

PART ONE

GOING OVER

Footprints in the sand
To here, to there, to Nowhere,
And a seagull flying.

Santa Cruz, CA
1984

Chapter 1

BEFORE GOING OVER

Though the stream is deep
It wanders in a foggy haze.
I stumble unseeing.

It was an autumn afternoon in 1920. Dr. Lamson, a "lady doctor," had come to our house on Runnymeade Street, San Mateo County, California, to assist my mother in giving birth to her fourth child. All went well and I was born at three o'clock in the afternoon. Twenty minutes later, after the doctor had already left, my mother was sitting up in bed eating an apple when she realized that another baby was coming! My dad got on a bicycle to try to fetch the doctor again. I don't think he ever did catch up with her. In the meantime, my aunt Lily was there and assisted in the birth of my twin sister Marguerite 35 minutes after I was born. This happened on Halloween, October 31, 1920. Ever since then, my twin and I have never been able to decide who was the trick and who was the treat. What I can say, though, is that 35 minutes was quite important for me as *older* brother.

I'm writing about all this, first, I guess, because it is an interesting story in itself, but also because it brings up the matter of my start in life.

Early Years

This book is mainly about what began happening to me when I arrived in Japan in 1953. However, the time before I went to Japan had a deep influence on this happening, so we'd better begin with these formative years. It seems that our mother really did not want any more children. She already had three, and was busy trying to raise them. There was also the problem of her age—she was over forty. Now, I deeply loved my mother and still do, and I profoundly respected her as a person. There was real heroism in her life. But ever since I heard about the power of prenatal influence at a holistic health conference in San Diego in 1970, I've strongly suspected that a feeling of not being wanted affected me even before I was born and was not erased by the love we twins subsequently received from our mother and the rest of the family.

I hear that they quite enjoyed bringing us up. But it's certain that for many years I labored under very poor self-esteem. Such feelings created many protective barriers around me and have interfered with my ability to relate to people. How could people take me seriously? I just couldn't feel that they could. I always seemed to start out below others, inferior to them. Those feelings were also, I feel, a primary cause for my arrested consciousness.

Actually, I was just an ordinary kid of my time, but quite mixed up. I was nine years old when the Great Depression hit. My father already had tuberculosis. I'm sure it was terrible for him not to be able to continue as the breadwinner for our family of seven. In fact, when he began to get well after his first treatment at Beresford Hospital, he left the hospital too early so he could get back to work. The disease returned so seriously that he never got his strength back, and he died when I was only nineteen. As a result, my mother ended up taking in boarders. This must have been terribly hard on the daughter of a well-to-do English family. She scrimped and saved, but we were basically poor.

For someone with already precariously low self-esteem, this was a serious problem. I was really ashamed of our poverty, and hid it in every way I could. And, of course, I also hid my feelings about the situation. This was especially true during the two years I spent at St. Joseph's Military Academy in Belmont, California, after Marguerite and I graduated from public grade school.

Our mother wanted us to get some Catholic education, so she squared her shoulders and went to talk to the Sisters of Mercy, who ran the school. Always so generous, they let me in to St. Joseph's for basically nothing. There were a lot of fairly rich kids there. My best friend in those days, Harry Tuckey, lived in St. Francis Woods, one of the finest residential areas in San Francisco. You can imagine what this did to my feelings about myself and to the development of my abilities to relate to others. It was rather like being under a constant state of siege. I always had to keep up my guard so people wouldn't find out about my poverty and what I was really like.

Adding to this was the fact that I got quite mixed up and badly oppressed by the super-strict moral teachings of the Catholic Church of those days. At times, I was terrified that I would go to hell. This was an excruciatingly lonely and frightening feeling.

Arrested Consciousness

As I grew into my teens, I couldn't come up with anything that I clearly wanted to be. When I was in high school and people asked me about this, I'd say, "maybe I'll become an architect." But I wasn't at all sure. This uncertainty just added to my low self-esteem and my general, though well-hidden, malaise. It's no wonder I wasn't able to open myself up to full consciousness of whatever I was engaged in at the moment.

I suspect that this is why I have so few memories of my childhood. I'm always amazed during our family gatherings when I hear my brother or sisters recalling so many details of the years when we were growing together. I just don't remember. The same is true of my 15 years of training as a Jesuit. Here too, as I hear Jesuit classmates talk and recall, there's so much I seem to have missed out on. I know I was there, but I wasn't there with enough awareness to recall the events.

My childhood and youth went on in a kind of vague way, except for one thing: I've always been interested in God! This also means that I've always been interested in the pilgrim path to God—that is, spirituality. Inside, my heart was made for God, and it was restless until it began to find some "rest in God."[1] The famous quote from St. Augustine on which this last sentence is based has been very meaningful to me ever since my mother first taught it to me when I was a child. Down deep, I couldn't seem to really get interested in anything else. There was never anything else that I could give my whole self to. And since I was never clear on what my path to God would be, I remained vague and indecisive.

Finally, during my first two years of high school at St. Joseph's, I dreamily determined that I would become a Trappist brother at Gethsemane Abbey in Kentucky. This gave me a certain, though hidden, focus until my senior year at Bellarmine College Preparatory in San Jose, California, a Jesuit school. At that time, the Trappist life seemed to lose its luster for me. Part of the problem was that even in this matter of a vocation, I was not sure of myself. I just didn't have the decisiveness to take the steps necessary to actually go to Gethsemane. As usual, I procrastinated and kept ruminating in my head.

On the other hand, a number of my classmates were thinking of entering the Jesuits. It sounded so much easier than all the hassle connected with the Trappist route that I finally decided to tag along with them. Even this entailed all the agonies of coming to a decision. I listed all the reasons for and against, but that didn't work. Finally, in the summer of 1938, I just followed my gut feeling and went. In spite of some very low times and some surface doubts and discontent, deep down I've always known it was the right decision.

Jesuit Training

My two years as a novice and a further two years studying Latin, Greek, and the humanities were spent at the Sacred Heart Novitiate, Los Gatos, California. In spite of occasional obsessive scrupulosity attacks taking over my poor, tentative mind, I was basically happy. I was on a spiritual path. I remember a visit from two of the Mercy Sisters who had taught me at St. Joseph's. One of them, Sister M. Madeleine, asked what I hoped to do as a Jesuit. My immediate response was, "Novice Master"! I vaguely remember her somewhat surprised little laugh as she reacted. I'm sure that she thought that in my enthusiasm I was being presumptuous and a bit proud. What I meant, though, was simply that I was really interested in spirituality.

About twelve years later, when I was facing ordination to the priesthood, the old indecision came to center stage again. I knew that being a priest had never been my main attraction. It was religious life as a spiritual path that I was interested in. The only way I could settle my doubts about being ordained was to say to myself that I'd tried to do God's will all these years and now I'm led to this, so it must be God's will. The main memory that stands out from the ordination ceremony in St. Mary's Cathedral in San Francisco is a scriptural phrase used somewhere in the liturgy: "You have not chosen me. I have chosen you." My other memory is that, in spite of there being 26 men ordained, from the moment we entered the Cathedral to the time we processed out, it only took exactly one hour! Actually, all was done beautifully, but I've sometimes thought that such extraordinary speed might deserve a place in some ecclesiastical book of records.

After our theology studies came a final nine months of spiritual training called tertianship. It was during this time that the course of my life was decided. People sometimes ask me why I went to Japan. I usually explain that in the generous enthusiasm of my novitiate days I had volunteered to go to China. That was the mission field of the California Jesuits at that time. I had never revoked that offering. Now, in tertianship, the call came for volunteers to go to Japan to help start a school in Hiroshima. Something definitely clicked in me. I wasn't much interested in starting a school, even in Hiroshima, but the part about Japan pulled me.

This time I didn't spend a lot of time on the pros and cons. I just followed my gut feeling and wrote to the Province Superior saying that I'd like to change my volunteer assignment from China to Japan. During our final eight-day retreat in May of 1953, I received an official letter assigning me to the Japan Project. At once, I wrote to all my family. The public announcement was made on Pentecost Sunday, May 25. That evening, I went over to preside at Benediction (a devotional service) at the convent of the Sisters' hospital next door to our Tertianship house. Kneeling there before the altar, I just knew that it was right. I wasn't meant to go to China; I was meant to go to Japan. I remember how good it felt to be sure about something important. And over the years, nothing in my life has been more certain.

One final recollection from those last days in tertianship is revealing. I said to myself, "I'm ready to direct retreats now." This may not seem like much, but it was quite a statement for me at the time. I was being clear and definite. Note, too, that it was in the area of spirituality. Sure enough, my commitment was tested right away. Tertianship ended about June first, and I spent that summer in San Francisco getting ready to go to Japan. One afternoon, I'd been downtown shopping and had come back late to the University of San Francisco, where I was staying. There was an urgent message from the Provincial Superior asking me if I could pinch-hit at an eight-day retreat for the B.V.M. Sisters up at Petaluma, California. The Jesuit from Oregon who had come down to direct the retreat had dropped dead on Market Street in San Francisco. So I went. It seems that the Provincial had said to the Sister something like, "Don't worry. I'll take care of the retreat," so they were expecting him! No wonder the Sister who met me at the door that evening kept looking over my shoulder for someone else. She was clearly not expecting such a young, immature director. But actually, things did go pretty well and the Sisters seemed to get a lot out of the week.

Unpacking

As I write about these early years, I realize that I am unpacking them. From where I now stand many years later, I am able to see much better than I could at the time what was actually happening. I could never have written this way about those events at the time they happened. I simply wasn't conscious enough. Thanks, though, to the miracle of memory, the form and energy of all those events can be revisited and reinterpreted. I propose now to turn to my years in Japan and to engage in the same interpretative review as I try to unpack my whole process of "going over."

Chapter 2

GOING OVER

The misty river
Turns East and I begin
To see my face.

I t was an early August morning in 1953 when the Norwegian cargo ship the *Pleasantville* sailed through the Golden Gate of San Francisco Bay heading for Manila, Hong Kong, and Yokohama. On board, I took a Dramamine to get me through the rough waters outside the Gate and settled in for a four-week trip to Japan. My companions were three Jesuits bound for Japan and one for Taiwan. It was thus that I began the greatest adventure of my life, an adventure that would last twenty-nine years.

A Consciousness Adventure

I was close to 33 years old, an age when most people have already completed their youthful travels and have begun to settle down. I was just beginning. I've always seemed to be a slow starter. It's been clear to me for years that mine was a case of arrested consciousness, and I feel that I was never quite fully conscious until I had spent a good amount of time in Japan. This actually makes sense, because the quest I began that morning in August was a consciousness adventure. (Although, of course, I wasn't conscious of this at that time.)

The most striking event on that initial voyage came at the very end. The ship had stopped at Hong Kong to unload some cargo. The work was done in haste and we left port earlier than scheduled, because a typhoon was coming up from the south. The storm's name was Rita. Well, Rita followed us at a distance all the way to Japan. After we docked at Yokohama, Father "Buck" Forster, S.J., drove the four of us in a jeep down to the Jesuit language school in Yokosuka. The very next day, Rita hit the Kanto area (Tokyo and surroundings) with full force. In fact, the eye of the huge storm passed right over Yokosuka. Did this natural event have any special meaning? Who's to say? But for me, it now means that I had arrived at the place where my inner eye would finally be opened.

The typhoon cleaned out the atmosphere of the whole Kanto. The day after was blessed with a pure, deep blue sky. I climbed up a tiny hill on the language school property and for the first time in my life saw Mount Fuji. Fuji-San is the glory of the land we call Japan. Again, for me, seeing it was a sign that it was through the beauty of this gracious land—as well as the whole culture and consciousness of the Japanese people—that I would come to see Beauty itself.

Years later, I was down in Sasebo, near Nagasaki, directing a retreat for some Good Shepherd Sisters from Australia. The retreat stretched from late in December to the beginning of January. After a day or two into the New Year, the Emperor and his family had their annual public audience with a goodly crowd of ordinary folks. I watched it on T.V. When the brief meeting was over, the television reporter asked one elderly lady for her reaction to the audience. "Tasukaremashite!" she exclaimed, "Tasukaremashite!" This translates as "I was saved!" (or helped, or rescued). Ever since then, this is what I've always said about my experience in Japan,

"Tasukaremashite!" The Japanese consciousness in general, and in particular my contact with Buddhism, has totally changed my life, made me into a better, richer human, and revitalized my Christianity.

A Better Christian

Direct and intimate contact with Buddhism didn't actually begin for me until 1969. One incident from that initial year fits in perfectly here. I had been going to the *zendo* (meditation hall) in Kamakura for about three months when I was granted *shoken* (*sho* = mutual, *ken* = seeing). In this simple ceremony, I formally met the zen master Yamada Koun Roshi and was accepted as his disciple in all things pertaining to zen. Actually, Yamada Roshi was still called Sensei (Teacher) at that time. He was gradually taking over the direction of the Kamakura zendo from its founder Yasutani Roshi.

Three of us went into the Sensei's room together for a simple ceremony and then were interviewed individually. The Sensei's question to me was, "What is your *kokorozashi*?" (Your aspiration or intention in entering the zen path.) I wasn't very clear about this. My life still abounded in vagueness. In going to the zendo, I hadn't followed my head at all. I'd obeyed a gut feeling, so I had no ready answer to the question. I finally blurted out something about *togo*, integration. Well, the Sensei didn't quite understand what I meant and neither did I. For some reason, I went on to say that I was a Catholic Christian. That I intended to live and die as such. But that I really felt zen was important for me. "Oh," said Yamada Sensei. "Yes. Remember that there are two kinds of zen. There's Buddhist Zen with all its teachings, images, chants, etc. Then there's just zen, which goes with any religion. You just do zen and you will become a better Christian."

Yamada Roshi was a big man, both physically and spiritually. His heart was broad and his insight true. With that shoken, I formally entered a path that, just as he said, was to transform my Christianity. Looking back now, I realize clearly that my problem, as a Christian, was that I was too much in my head. My spiritual path was intellectual rather than experiential. This was brought home to me as late as 1964 by the strange surprise I felt at some words I read.

Toward Consciousness

I was standing on the platform of the old wooden station of the Taura district of Yokosuka waiting for the familiar cream-and-blue Yokosuka Line train, reading a small book by the theologian Karl Rahner titled *Nature and Grace*. Rahner was arguing against "the widespread view of grace" as "a supernature above man's *conscious* spiritual and moral life."[1] He said that it's not surprising "when a man takes very little interest in this mysterious superstructure of his being; this grace is not present where he is present to himself in his *immediate self-awareness*."[2] Rahner maintained that instead the movements of grace are a real part of one's conscious existence; that these "existential facts" of his concrete (his "historical") nature are not just accidents of his being beyond his consciousness, but make themselves apparent *"in his experience of himself."*[3] (Italics in these quotations added.)

Even now, after all these years, I can still remember the impact these words had on me on that station platform and afterward. To say that we can and should be *conscious* of grace in our daily lives opened up a whole new level of life to me. Rahner was speaking about direct experience, "immediate self-awareness." It seemed as if all my life I had been thinking *about* these things. Especially during my three years of philosophical and four years of theological training, I had studied and learned all about grace. However, the realities dealt with in all those studies had remained just ideas. Above all, *supernatural* grace, essential as it was deemed, had always seemed far above and beyond any direct experience.

Some years later, when Thomas Merton spoke in Anchorage as he left the U.S. for the last time, he said very simply that the Church in the U.S. is too cerebral. Well, I was certainly a product of my time in this regard. For years and years I lived mainly in my head, in my intellect. My approach to life was to analyze, categorize, and define. None of these operations of the mind can bring one to *immediate* awareness, which is the only experience that transforms us. Between feeling that I was no good and my inability to easily fit into ordinary social life, staying in my head was a nice, safe retreat. It definitely arrested my direct and forceful consciousness of events.

As I reflect now, very little of my training, not just in philosophy and theology but even in spirituality, really took for me. I just wasn't there enough for it to actually form me. Much of it was just water off the duck's back. I was too busy protecting my little old self to be consciously transformed, but at a deep level the changes were happening.

Even as a child, I can remember how *reason* was taught to me as foremost. Once at the dinner table the subject of the Irish came up. Both my mother and father agreed that the Irish were too emotional. They were not governed by reason. Following one's intellect was of primary value. Now, years later, I treasure my Celtic roots and admire the superb intellectual heritage of Celtic culture. I often brag, with a hiccup, that I have a fourth of scotch in me. (I know that should be Scot, but to be correct would spoil the *bon mot*.) I've even gone so far as to investigate and discover that grandmother Moody's family is a sept of the Steward clan. The fact remains, however, that I was profoundly influenced by the rationalism of the first half of the twentieth century.

Certainly in recent years the Christian church and Western society are becoming more balanced between thought and direct experience. Nevertheless, I believe there is still the tendency in the West to overvalue our differentiating intellect to the detriment of immediate, existential experience. So to drive the point home and to make even clearer my own need for the revitalization that direct experience brings, I'll borrow a story from Fr. Tony DeMello, S.J., a truly great talker and storyteller. I can't remember where he situated the tale. I'll locate it in Japan.

A little boy and his father are on a walk in the hills of Kamakura one fine spring day. Suddenly, off in the woods to the left of their path a bird begins to sing and trill beautifully. The little boy is entranced. "Oh! Singing! Bird singing!" the boy exclaims and stops to listen, totally absorbed. The father smiles and stops too. Then he begins to explain that the bird is an *uguisu*, a Japanese nightingale. That it is a shy bird that one is rarely able to glimpse. That it is brown with no brilliant coloration. That it only sings this way during the spring months. That it...etc., etc. The boy turns to listen to the father tell him all *about* the bird, and the ecstasy of the direct experience is gone.

I would ask if it not true that even today, not only my life but most of Christianity still needs renewal in the matter of immediate experience of ourselves in God.

I recall the frustration I used to feel when reciting the psalms. Walking up and down in my room in Kamakura, I would even get angry when a psalm came up that kept praising God for all the wonderful things "He" has done for us. The praying was just a mental exercise. I didn't feel either the wonderful things or the praise and gratitude. I wasn't really happy and fulfilled, because there was so little experience of God in my life. Again, one of the greatest obstacles to this experience was that my constant approach to life was looking *at*, thinking and judging *about*.

Looking back over my first forty years of life, I now feel that it was a blessing of Providence that I was too much closed up in guarding myself to be really formed by all the training I received. In effect, I was left open to be formed by the Buddhist and Shinto consciousness of Japan. I was able to "go over" in a deeper way. All the vagueness, confusion, and even pain now turned to immense gratitude.

Chapter 3

INTO ZEN

Three Clouds Zendo

The bells and incense
Measure long hours
Of pain and peace

Although the Japanese consciousness fascinated me from my very first days in Japan, my first inkling of an attraction to Zen Buddhism came unexpectedly while I was teaching at our Junior-Senior High School, Hiroshima Gakuin, on the outskirts of Hiroshima.

Zen Beginnings

The new school had only two years' of Junior High at the time. The whole student body plus the teachers were on an *ensoku* (outing) in the form of a hike in the hills behind the city. I don't know how it happened, but in the little group I was in, the subject of zen came up. Immediately, one very sharp little youngster leaped up onto a flat rock beside the path and sat down in a perfect lotus position, the favored posture of *zazen* (sitting zen). His grace, spontaneity, and sudden stillness struck me so powerfully that his image is still with me after almost 40 years. At the same time, a vague but strong longing to do zazen arose in my heart. A seed was planted that only began to sprout nine years later.

By then, I had transferred from Hiroshima to our Japanese language school near Tokyo. The new school building/residence was still under construction at Kamakura, so we were living in a retreat house at Kamishakujii on the outskirts of Tokyo. It was there, early in 1965, that I was privileged to read the English manuscript of Fr. Hugo Lasalle's little book, *Zen, The Path of Enlightenment*. As a great pioneer, Fr. Lasalle, S.J., had been practicing zazen seriously for many years. Now he was sharing some of his experience. On the strength of the inspiration from this book, I tried some sitting all on my own. It didn't go well at all. My legs hurt after only a few minutes. My mind was all over the place. I did try, but before long gave it up.

In May of that year, we moved into the new language school at Juniso, Kamakura, just one hour by train west by southwest of Tokyo. Finally, in April three years later, I walked down the Juniso hill and on along the narrow road to the old temple Jomyoji. At last I was beginning the zen path. I was nervous, confused, even somewhat afraid, but something made me go. My gut feeling was leading me out of my head. The assault on my cerebral castle had finally begun in earnest.

The Primacy of Experience

In the zendo the *primacy of direct experience* was insisted upon at all times, both in practice and in teaching. We were also constantly warned against the intellectual approach to life as ultimately fruitless and completely inadequate. I had lots of trouble understanding the special zen language, but in spite of that and many other difficulties, the message came through strong and clear. I was being challenged to change. It was a whole different world than that from which I had gotten my training thus far, and I recognized it as something I longed for. The goal was nothing less than direct experience of the very Source of life.

Of course, Jesuit training accepted the primacy of experience. In the Spiritual Exercises of Ignatius, our founder, the term for true experience is the Latin word *consolatio*. And the primary purpose of all Jesuit ministry is to communicate this "consolation" to others. But as I see our training now, in practice the accent was in some ways overwhelmingly on the mental. One climax of the whole program was a two-hour oral examination covering all that philosophy and theology had to say *about* reality. True, the training ended with the nine months of tertianship—"a school of affection" (*schola affectus*), a time given over to the revitalization of the experiential character of one's life. But for me, at least, it didn't really take. I remained pretty much high and dry in my head.

In the zendo, Miyazaki Sensei, one of the main assistants to the zen master, taught me the customary practice for beginners, the counting of one's breath. I was put to counting my exhalations from one to ten to the exclusion of everything else. While the physical sitting was difficult, the inner discipline was even harder. I attended the two all-day *zazenkai* (zazen meetings) each month and did my best sitting at home. From the very beginning, and all during my six years of formal Zen training, I never felt like going to the zazenkai or to the periodic *sesshin* (retreats). It was always a struggle. But I did go, and deep down was happy that I did. I was changing.

We come here to a rather important point. I was in no way obliged to go. There was no semi-monthly obligation comparable to my Catholic "Sunday obligation." There was no legalism about it at all. Again, the whole focus was on experience. The message was: "If you want to break through to true realization, the zazenkai and sesshin are immense help. Do come."

All the zen teachers, because of their own experience, were eager to bring me to something similar. This is the bodhisattva spirit. They were not trying to convert me. They wanted me to come to experience, not to become a Buddhist as such. I can't help but contrast this with ordinary Christian drive to convert people to the Christian church, the *only* place where it is believed there is salvation and the experience of God. Even this direct experience of God is mainly relegated to heaven.

The pattern of instruction in the zendo was totally consistent with its basic goal. First came practical directions on how to sit. We were taught what to do both internally and externally. Inspiration and motivation to keep sitting were given by constantly holding up experiential examples of enlightenment. These were stories of real people, both from the past and of our present time. A basically good ethical life was also expected, but not dwelt on. The more philosophical and religious teachings of Buddhism were only treated in a very simple and basic way, when they were helpful to practice. Almost nothing was said about Buddhism as an institution with its own laws and authority structure.

A Different Kind of Teaching

Very early on in my time in the zendo, I felt the contrast between this model and our usual Catholic training, both of Church members and of prospective converts. The catechism begins with dogmas and creeds. Right from the start, the institutional Church, its liturgy, hierarchy, and laws are integral to the catechetical instruction. Obedience, loyalty, and belonging to the Church are strongly enjoined. Moral precepts are explained at length and forcibly prescribed. Personal practices of piety come toward the end of the process. As Beatrice Bruteau brings out in her fine book *What We Can Learn From the East*,[1] to some extent we must say that in Western religious practice, beliefs, attitudes, and behavior are considered means to becoming a true Christian. In the East, all such things—and even being a Christian or Buddhist—are simply means to the goal of ultimate Experience. I suspect that the order of instruction and initiation in the various non-Catholic churches may be different from what I have described, but I feel a basic contrast does remain, In the zendo, one didn't go to receive religious instruction as such. We went for practice leading to enlightenment.

Yamada Roshi was accustomed to teaching all this in a far more simple and graphic way. Many times he used the example of sugar. "You can know all about the color, the crystalline structure, the weight and chemical composition of sugar. But you do not actually know it until you experience even a tiny taste of it. Then you know sugar. So it is with reality."

From my own experience and from my knowledge of the paths of the Christians at the Kamakura zendo and other zen practitioners I've met, I can gratefully affirm that Buddhism in general and Zen in particular can help greatly to revitalize the experiential character of Christianity, bring new meaning to the communications of Christian experience, and even sharpen our creedal formulations and bring all these elements of Christ's church to be more consonant with the twenty-first century.

Chapter 4

DOKUSAN

Yamada Roshi

Seated on the Rock
The lighthouse shines into the dark
And restless waves.

Nothing stands out more powerfully in the memory of my years of formal zen training than *dokusan*. *Doku* means individual, private; *san* is to go in a humble way. So dokusan is going individually, sincerely, and humbly to the zen master for private direction. (In Rinzai Zen it's termed *sanzen*.) I went to Yamada Roshi for dokusan many times, and it was always an energizing, revitalizing encounter. Westerners would often try to use the brief time to ask some intellectual questions, clear up some nagging mental doubts. I tried to do this once or twice, but learned right off that it was not allowed. The Roshi absolutely refused to go into such matters. He was always and only interested in my level of insight. It was again a matter of the zen priority of experience. Dokusan was a time for *discernment*. The norm against which the Roshi checked my state of consciousness was not some creedal formula or theological system; the norm for discernment was his own experience.

Lineage and Discernment

The personal experience of Yamada Koun Roshi had been discerned and affirmed by his teacher Yasutani Hakuun Roshi. The validity of Yasutani Roshi's enlightenment had been affirmed by his teacher Harada Daiun Roshi. Ideally, this line of discernment and affirmation goes back from one teacher to another, all the way to Shakyamuni Buddha himself. Our immediate line of teachers is graphically represented in the very name of our small Kamakura zendo. Yamada Roshi was building the zendo at his own expense and on his own property—even joining it by corridors to his house—at the time when I entered zazenkai. When the new zendo was formally blessed and inaugurated in the fall of 1969, the Roshi's old friend Nakagawa Soen Roshi presided at the ceremony. It was then that Soen gave it the name Sanun Zendo, the Three Clouds Zen Hall. *Un* (cloud) is in the name of all three of the roshis in our direct line: Daiun (Great Cloud), Hakuin (White Cloud), and Koun (Cultivation Cloud).

In theory, every zen practitioner should be able to trace his or her line of transmission directly back to Shakyamuni. There certainly have been many times that a master arose not so much out of the influence of a teacher as from his or her own existential questioning—together, perhaps, with help from the enlightened Buddhist sutras. But even these mavericks, if they were to publicly teach zen, had to have their experience checked and affirmed. From beginning to end, zen stands or falls on the teacher's discernment.

Inka-shomei (often just *inka*) is an authentic seal of certification. In effect, it is a teaching certificate. It is only given to a student when the teacher discerns that the student has both authentic enlightenment and the knowledge of zen practices and teachings adequate for transmitting zen to others. Once again, the main requisite for this certification is that of insightful experience of the True Nature of Reality. If a master were to give inka to a student who had no genuine enlightenment, that line of transmission would end up empty and deceitful.

So serious is this that some masters, to their infinite sorrow, have simply let their line die out without a successor, rather than cause its corruption. Other lines have dried up precisely because teachers gave inka to unworthy disciples. The students might be sons of old temple classmates of the teacher who are needed to take over the temples from their fathers, so they are simply passed through the system. The result is a lifeless kind of zen, useful in a social way, but lacking the true inner spirit. I heard that this kind of situation was the main reason Yasutani Roshi and Harada Roshi moved out to the margin of their own zen line.

In all this, the vital importance of true dokusan is obvious. It is precisely through the intimate discernment of numerous dokusan periods that a master can trace the development of a student and ultimately come to the assurance that he or she can give inka to that student.

"Stop the boat" Koan

From the start, I was well aware of what a profound event dokusan was. Of all those treasured times, there is one that stands out in a special way. It took place after I had begun koan study.

A *koan* is an anecdote or saying that transmits a zen master's enlightenment. The one I had been given went something like this: "See that boat out there on the water about 100 yards from shore? Standing on the shore, stop that boat." Somehow the koan clicked within me right away. I felt confident about it and enjoyed it. A week or so later, I went up to Tokyo for the evening zazenkai with the Roshi. Going into the dokusan room was always like entering a charged energy field. I made the usual bows and announced the koan I was working with. The Roshi smiled, looked at me intently, and even leaned forward in anticipation. With my own body, I demonstrated my experience of the koan. The Roshi leaned back nodding and smiled broadly. He indicated his approval and even got up to give a more expansive demonstration of the koan's insight. With this, the energy of the room was lifted to even greater heights. The room was filled with light—that light which has been communicated down through centuries and centuries of disciplined practice and existential experience. The very process of discernment, which arose out of the personal enlightenment of the Roshi himself, carried me to greater light. The Roshi gave me the next koan and then dismissed me. I walked on air back to the meditation room.

Thus it was that the experiential basis of my life was building up. Why had my consciousness been so arrested? There are many reasons, both personal and societal. As to the latter, I can't help but feel that the Christianity I grew up in was far more interested in going out to share Christ with others than in the actual direct experience of Christ. I suppose I must say that in many ways, in my times, Christianity has been more missionary than visionary.

Zen Sensitivity

I cannot close this chapter without dwelling once again on the intense spiritual sensitivity present in the dokusan room, especially in the teacher. During a sesshin or a zazenkai, when the signal for dokusan is given, everyone rushes to line up behind a bell placed not far from the door to the teacher's room. Every time the teacher is ready for another dokusan disciple, he or she rings a little bell inside the room. The first person in line responds by ringing the bell outside and proceeds with the appropriate bows into the dokusan room. It is said, and I believe it, that a true master can tell the spiritual state of a student just by the sound of the bell that the student has rung.

Another example of zen sensitivity is found in a beautiful koan featuring the famous ninth-century master Joshu (Chinese, Chao Chou).

Joshu went to a hermit's hut and asked, "Anybody in? Anybody in?" The hermit thrust up his fist. Joshu said, "The water is too shallow for a ship to anchor." Thereupon he left.

Again he went to a hermit's hut and asked, "Anybody in? Anybody in?" The hermit thrust up his fist. Joshu said, "Here is freedom to give, to take away, to kill, to give life." He made a profound bow.

Mumonkan #11 (Author's translation)[1]

Of course, Joshu's question "Anybody in?" is an inquiry about the level of self-identification (enlightenment) that the hermits have reached. It amounts to, "Is the True Self-consciousness here?" Both hermits answer the same way, by thrusting up a fist. In the first case, the gesture is discerned as inadequate. The True Self is simply not spontaneously manifested in the gesture. The master moves on. In the second, the very same gesture is seen as a clear manifestation of the one Source, who does all things freely (giving, taking away, killing, giving life, etc.) In the total spontaneity and complete confidence of the hermit's gesture, Joshu had all he needed to measure the depth of the disciple. Such discernment takes profound sensitivity born of true personal experience.

It is a beautiful thing that the tiny hidden event related in this koan from a T'ang dynasty Zen temple has echoed in zen halls for over a thousand years and still draws us toward the advanced consciousness so purely and powerfully developed in the hearts of true zen practitioners—an enlightened consciousness guarded only by piercing discernment.

Chapter 5

PRACTICE

Ohenro

Trudging alone
To this one and to temples everywhere
Along with everyone.

Asmall group of us had gone for a picnic to Goshiki no Hama (Five Color Beach) on the Pacific coast of Shikoku, the smallest of the main islands of Japan. We were hurrying back to the city of Kochi, when we passed the steps leading up to a Buddhist temple on the top of a wooded hill. As ever, I felt the familiar pull. I've always been deeply attracted to Buddhist temples and Shinto shrines. Another sign of my God fascination, I'd say. I said to the other, "it's too bad we're in such a hurry. I'd love to visit that temple. But it's okay," and walked on with the rest. Suddenly one lady said, "Nido konai kara, Shimpusama, itte irasshai." ("Please go ahead, Father, you'll never come here again.")

That was all the encouragement I needed. I backtracked a bit and started running up the stairs. Halfway up, I paused to look at a little waterfall on the left side that was obviously used for the ascetic practice of *takigyo*—standing under the cold water almost naked while reciting the sutras. Duly impressed and secretly attracted by this, I rushed on up the steps.

The Immovable Light King

As I charged over the top step, I almost ran into the more than life-sized statue right in front of the very modest temple. The figure was standing with a sword in one hand and a rope in the other. Flames of fire were portrayed all around him, and he had a fierce look on his face. At once I recognized Fudo Myoo, the Immovable Light King. I had met this figure many times before, and had always felt that he was just what I needed in my spiritual path. Even today, a five-inch statue of Fudo-San sits right here before me on my desk as I write this page.

Fudo Myoo is a personification of fierce and immovable determination. This bodhisattva figure is totally dedicated to bringing all beings to salvation. You can see this dedication in his ferociously intent face and eyes. The cosmic flames surrounding him illuminate the darkest confusion and burn away all evil passions. His sword defends the truth and cuts off all illusions. His rope pulls up those in distress and binds the evil movements of the human heart. In Tantric Buddhism, Fudo-San is a personification of the will of the cosmic buddha Dainichi, the Sun Buddha of supreme wisdom. Dainichi is the central figure in both Tendai and Shingon Buddhism in Japan. I didn't know all this when I first met the Immovable Light King in some of his many images all around the country. For me, he at once became the symbol of steadfast and unrelenting practice.

Henro

The temple where I stood was a pilgrimage temple. I had already heard of the Henro, the great pilgrimage path covering 88 temples all around the island of Shikoku. I was deeply attracted, but had no idea that I could ever actually make the pilgrimage. But there at Seiryuji, number 36 of the 88 temples, the image of Fudo-San hit me so powerfully that right then and there the attraction turned into an incipient resolve. *Why not make the Henro?*

Hen means general, everywhere. *Ro* is path, road. So *henro* is the path to everywhere or the universal path. In Japan, as in all lands, a pilgrimage is an archetypal event taking one to the Source. It is a spiritual practice that entails hardship, devotion, and detachment. But I had no clear or special purpose in doing the Henro. Once again, I just followed a gut attraction.

I don't even remember how we all got together, but in the summer of 1971, five of us began the pilgrimage from Ryozanji, Temple #1, at Naruto in northeast Shikoku. We were a group of three men and two women. A young French Jesuit and I were the two foreigners. As much as possible, we walked. But when there was a long distance between temples, we took a bus or train.

We almost always stayed at the temples, and were usually housed and fed quite well for a very modest sum. I had no problem sleeping on the floor, except when the futon was too thin. The one thing I never got used to was not having a chair to sit on. But this too, along with the hard, hot walking, the backpacks, the mosquitoes and bugs, the thirst and fatigue, was simply part of the ascetic practice.

On arriving at a temple, the custom is to first stand in front of the main building and recite the sutras and other prayers that you have already decided upon as your pilgrimage practice. After completing your devotions, you go to the office to have the temple attendant stamp your record book called a *nogyosho* (completed-one's-sutra recitation-book). I still have mine with all 88 temples registered. In our group we were all Catholics, so we didn't recite any Buddhist sutras, but I made it my practice to pray the first part of the third eucharistic prayer of the Mass, along with prayers for world peace and such intentions.

I will never forget the path from the eleventh temple to the twelfth. We walked almost all day up and down a steep mountain trail and crossed only one narrow, deserted dirt road. It was a marvelous treat just to be in nature. At the same time, however, we were surrounded by and accompanied by the thousands upon thousands who had walked this very path for hundreds of years. We often came upon statues of Jizo Bosatsu, the bodhisattva who is, among other things, the patron of travelers. And all along, we saw little strips of metal attached to branches of trees and bushes. On them were written words of encouragement and devotion, like "You are always with Kobo Daishi" (the great saint who traditionally originated the pilgrimage). There were also the equivalent of exhortations such as "Gambare" ("Hang in there"). Finally we arrived at Shosanji, Temple #12, one of the most beautiful and ethereal temples I have ever seen. Far up in the mountains, isolated except for a tiny village a short distance away, built on huge stone walls and surrounded by ancient trees, it was an oasis of natural spirituality.

Another memorable walk was the time we spent almost two full hours passing through a huge bamboo forest. The grace, the cleanness, the silence, and the powerful energy of the towering bamboo are all unforgettable. Such magic times, together with the spiritual energy of some temples and the hardships and fatigue, made the Henro into a transforming experience.

We met Fudo-San many times along the way and in the temples. The remark that the lady made that day of the picnic proved, happily, to be false; I actually did return again to Temple #36. In fact, I arrived there on a special feast day. The man in charge gave me a private explanation of the *gohonzon* (the main object of devotion) in the temple, a small statue of Namikiri Fudo. He related how Kobo Daishi had once calmed the waves by casting the statue into the sea during a storm.

We visited 24 temples that first summer. I returned the following summer and the next two springs to complete the pilgrimage. It took 40 days in all. Sometimes I was with others, sometimes alone. Saicho, one of the towering Japanese masters of spiritual discipline, speaks of a person with *doshin*. (*Do* = Way; *shin* = heart or inner reality.) Through the henro and through zen, I was gradually, though hardly perceptibly, beginning to be a doshin person. My mindset was changing. I was becoming set in *the way*. My very self-identity was becoming irrevocably altered. It was a real challenge for an introvert like myself to set out on such an adventure as the Henro, but it, too, turned out to be an important part of my going over.

Practices That Inspire

Close by Kyoto is Mt. Hiei, a large complex of five 2,500- to 3,000-foot peaks and many steep valleys. Hieizan stands guard over the ancient capital city at the most dangerous direction, the North East. It was with full cognizance of this danger that Saicho, the founder of Tendai Buddhism in Japan, began to build the huge monastic complex Enryakuji at the end of the eighth century. The founders of all the major Buddhist sects in the country trained at Hieizan; the only exceptions are Shingon, those sects earlier than Hieizan, and the very recent ones.

I've visited this mountain more than once and have been fascinated and impressed not only by the sheer size of the establishment, but also by its spiritual energy. For over twelve hundred years, Hieizan has been train-ing monks in an amazing variety of spiritual disciplines. I have a striking Japanese video called simply *Gyo* (Ascetical Practices) that presents many training practices currently being practiced in Japanese Buddhism. Mt. Hiei is featured in it.

Within the great Enryakuji complex is a small temple called Jogyodo, erected for a practice in honor of Amida Buddha. An Amida statue is seated in the middle of the room, and fills it with its presence. Day and night, the *gyoja* (practitioner) circumambulates the statue. His whole body, being, mind, and spirit are focused on the devotional mantra *Namu Amida Butsu* ("I venerate or praise Amida Buddha"), which he repeats out loud innumerable times. The monk pauses only for toilet breaks. He sits only for his meals and for two hours of sleep each day. Around the statue area is a bamboo railing for him to hang on to when he becomes dizzy.

At the beginning of our meditations at Mercy Center, we sometimes chant a simple mantra for 10 minutes or so. Even this short mantric repe-tition stops the inner dialogue and promotes quiet of mind. Imagine what

90 days and nights of continued mantric practice does to the gyoja's consciousness.

In nearby Hokkedo (Lotus Hall) temple, another gyoja is doing zen, seated without stirring in the lotus position for 90 days. Even his two hours of sleep are taken seated. Again, imagine the depth of meditation attainable in the absolute stillness of those three long months.

The video *Gyo* also shows the magnificent Shingon monastic center on Mt. Koya and the trainees there learning the *goma shiki* fire ceremony. This mystical rite goes all the way back to Vedic India (about 2000 B.C.E.) and is called *homa* in Sanskrit. Both Saicho and Kukai, the Shingon founder, brought it to Japan from their studies of Tantric Buddhism in China. It is an elaborate ritual in which oil, seeds, leaves, beans, incense, and wooden sticks are consumed in a fire at the center of an altar inside the temple building. On the sticks are written the prayers of the people who attend or ask for the ceremony. Although the rite is widely used in Japan as an intercessory ceremony in which people's prayers are offered up through the burning of the wooden prayer sticks, there is also a deep inner asceticism to the practice.

The performing monk engages in many exterior rites, but they all represent interior dispositions. There is inner visualization of various buddhas and bodhisattvas, among whom one very important figure is our old friend Fudo Myoo. All the exterior offerings and the interior representations are physically and psychologically put into the fire and consumed. Everything must drop off so that the participants can *jobutsu* (realize buddhahood in themselves). The egos of the monk and of those in attendance, together with all created things, are burnt up and returned to the Source, to be reborn as purified manifestations of the Source.

In the video, we also see a Shingon monk reciting a mantra in honor of the Bodhisattva Kokuzo 20,000 times each day for 50 days. We are shown the gyoja seated, fingering his counting beads as his lips barely move in recitation. I've never seen a more spiritual face than that of this monk. It rivals the face of a Tibetan monk I met once in Nepal who had just completed a three-year retreat.

All of the many and varied practices presented in *Gyo*, and all the less spectacular disciplines that make up Japanese Buddhism, have as their one inner purpose becoming a Buddha through enlightenment. Experience is absolutely primary, and therefore practice is essential. One technical term for the ultimate goal of the developmental process is *kensho-jobutsu* (seeing Reality – becoming a Buddha). Although this is mainly a zen term, it describes the very heart of all the many practices. These disciplines have been refined and refined down the centuries. When performed wholeheartedly, they can and do accomplish the intended transformation. In tantric terms, Fudo Myoo is still powerfully at work even in our times.

Sakai Yusai is an *ajari* (saintly master). In fact, he is an ajari twice over, because in 1986 he completed his second *sen-nichi-kai-ho-gyo* (literally, 1000-day-encircling-the–peaks practice). Anyone who accomplishes this gyo is called an ajari. People all over Japan were watching on television the day Ajari Sakai completed this amazing ascetic feat for the second time. This extraordinary practice is certainly the most spectacular of all the many varieties of gyo on Hieizan. It basically consists of walking/running what can perhaps best be described as a marathon course. But the course is not nicely level. It's all around and up and down the steep peaks and valleys of Mt. Hiei. There are two basic routes, one about 19 miles and the other about 25 miles. Ajari Sakai chose the longer one.

The practice is usually spread out over seven years. The gyoja runs one of the courses for 100 days in succession in four of the seven years, and 200 days in the other three years. In the sixth year, the course becomes 37.5 miles long, and for 100 days of the 200 in year seven the gyoja runs an astounding 52.5 miles each morning before breakfast! (Actually, the monk does take a bowl of miso soup or a rice ball or two before starting out.) It takes at least seven to nine hours of running up and down the steep valleys and along mountain ridges in all weather conditions, even heavy rain or snow. Absolutely nothing is an excuse to stop or to rest even one day. If the daily practice is interrupted, the whole gyo is cancelled.

There are over 250 stations along the way—temples, Shinto shrines, graves, special trees, rocks, and waterfalls. At each station, the appointed prayers, mantras, and mudras (ritual hand symbols) are offered. Each gyoja has to learn the special way of running without which the practice is impossible. He must run with total attention, at a steady pace, and in rhythm with the Fudo Myoo mantra which he is continually reciting. The gyojas speak of a special power that takes over. Otherwise, how could they manage such an extraordinary marathon?

In the fifth year, after 700 days of the circumambulation, the gyoja enter *doiri*. This is a deliberate near-death experience. Sequestered in a temple called Myoodo, the monk sits chanting sutras and reciting the Fudo mantra over 11,000 times a day for nine full days. He takes no food, no water, no sleep, no rest. In the invitation the gyoja sends to the other Hieizan monks for a final meal before the doiri, the monk announces his goal: "This foolish monk vows to commit himself wholeheartedly to the nine-day fast, purifying body and mind, hoping to become one with the Great Holy One, Fudo Myoo. Please join me for a farewell dinner."[1] Hakozaki Bunno, who was born in 1892 and lived well into his nineties, was one of the most tireless devotees of the kai-ho-gyo. Beyond even that, he underwent the nine-day fast an astounding 36 times. He used to say out of his own incredible experiences, "The purpose of gyo is to discover the joy of life."[2] There is a traditional proverb which declares, "To a practitioner of Tendai, everything is wonderful."

Chapter 6

ZAZEN

Kyosaku (Wake up Stick)

In the MU-ing hall
The monkey mind is silenced
By the kyosaku crash.

It's five o'clock in the morning on the fifth day of the *rohatsu sesshin*. This is the week-long zen retreat celebrated annually in our zendo from December first to the morning of December eighth, the morning that Shakyamuni came to full enlightenment upon seeing the Morning Star shining down on his bodhi tree. It's a cold morning in Kamakura. The breath of the sitters near the open doors is condensing into clouds here in the Three Clouds Zendo. Getting up, putting the bedding up into the cupboard, washing, stretching exercises—all these preparations are done. We sit down in two lines facing the side walls. Silence descends on the zendo. The new day of zazen has begun.

After a few minutes, Miyazaki Sensei quietly announces into the silence, "Kentan!" (*ken* = see; *tan* = the space where each one is sitting, one tatami mat.) The absolute stillness continues, except for a firm step that begins by the door and proceeds behind each one of us. Yamada Roshi has come to see us, to encourage us, to help us start the day, to add his powerful presence to the already vital energy of the hall. It is a magical moment. Often, there are only the silent steps. Sometimes, he clears his throat in his characteristic way. Now and then, he corrects this person's posture or encourages that person by a tap on the shoulder. We are facing a day of about ten hours of sitting and we need all the added strength we can get.

In zen, as in all great spiritual traditions, the primary discipline is mindfulness—being attentive to the here and now with bare, non-judgmental awareness. This is a 24-hour-a-day practice. But the special discipline of zen is, of course, zazen, which is nothing but mindfulness within a very limited, simple sphere of activity—sitting.

Dhyanna is a Sanskrit word meaning, in general, any absorbed state of mind brought about through concentrated awareness. It is mindfulness par excellence. The Indian monk Bodhidharma brought this mindfulness discipline to China in the sixth century. There, dhyanna became pronounced *ch'anna* or simply *ch'an* or *chen*. When it moved into Japan, the word became *zen*. Zazen is simply sitting zen.

Mu

Return again to those 30 or more people sitting so powerfully in the Sanun Zendo during the rohatsu sesshin. The zendo itself is very close to the famous Kamakura Daibutsu (Great Buddha statue), who has been sitting there in immensely impressive meditation for over six centuries. The figure is facing toward our zendo, and I often thought of how we were literally sitting at the feet of the Buddha.

Each person is sitting perfectly still just like the Buddha, with the trunk of the body erect and balanced. But what are we doing inside? Some of us may be fixing our attention on our breathing or even counting exhalations from one to ten. This practice is usually the only one followed until shoken.

Even after that, we would sometimes return to it in order to "re-collect" our-selves. At shoken, the Roshi almost invariably assigned the student "MU." This December morning, quite a number are engaged with a koan. The rest of us are "doing MU." The practitioner gives total attention to saying the syl-lable MU, which is repeated to the rhythm of the breath. Usually there is one long MUUUU to each exhalation. Basically, that's all there is to it. The prac-tice actually arises out of the most used koan in all zen:

> A monk in all seriousness asked Joshu, "Has a dog the Buddha-nature or not?" Joshu responded, "Mu!"
>
> Mumonkan #1 (Author's translation)[1]

So the practice is to ask oneself what the zen master Joshu is indicating by his one-syllable answer. *Mu* (Wu in Joshu's Chinese) is a negative, like non-, in-, or un- in English. *Mugen* means unlimited. But it is useless, in fact counterproductive, to think and reason about the koan, so we end up just repeating MU. This repetition of MU—either out loud or silently—is not much of an object for the attention, but it is an excellent example of zen with an object, meditation with form.

Yamada Roshi assigned and explained MU to me at shoken and I began the practice with enthusiasm. The attention to breathing that I had been practicing had not gone too well. MU at once turned out to be no less difficult. Corralling the monkey mind was one of the most strenuous strug-gles I've ever tried. My mental apparatus just wouldn't stand for concentra-tion on nothing but the weird syllable MU. Or perhaps I should say it sim-ply wouldn't stand still *on* it. The struggle went on for five years. And yes, it's still going on.

I'd go to dokusan embarrassed by my inability to maintain attention and the Roshi would smile and say, "Minna so desu, Shimpsu-San. Hitoiki, hitoiki de gambari nasai." ("Everyone's like that, Father. Keep on just one breath, one breath at a time.") At other times, when I reported a more quiet mind, he'd say, "Yoshi. MU to hitotsu ni nari nasai." ("Good. Become one with MU.")

I'd leave dokusan encouraged and sometimes, yes, everything would start to turn into MU. An airplane would fly overhead. Its motor sounded out MU. In *kinhin* (walking meditation), each step turned into MU. Just sitting was MU; eating was MU, or better yet, MU muing MU. This is quite a psychological state. Sometimes it is compared to the absorption a lover has toward the beloved.

One time, a Japanese Sister and a young Catholic lady came to our residence at Juniso to have a light dinner before going to the zendo for a sesshin. The lady in all simplicity stated that she was sure she would come to *kensho* (the first experience of enlightenment) during the retreat. We admonished her a bit, because that wasn't supposed to be the correct attitude. But she did go into a fine state in the course of the sesshin. It was then that Miyazaki Sensei told her to become absorbed in MU as in a beloved. She did, and came to an excellent breakthrough.

Focusing on MU actually does quiet the mind, because there is no *thought* about anything, just attention to this crazy syllable. The advantage of this non-meaning focus of attention is well pointed out in something that Yamada Roshi repeated many times: "Words with meaning are dead. Words without meaning are alive." Words with meanings are dead in the sense that they are fixed, static, and bounded. They do not point beyond themselves to the Unlimited. Even words like Infinite, Absolute, or Ultimate are concepts *about*. They entice us to think about them. Words without meaning are alive because they are unbounded, open, and dynamic. If we give total attention to them, they can quiet the mind and open us out to direct experience of the Infinite.

Quiet!

You will notice how many times I have used the expression "quiet the mind." One of the most enlightened people I have ever known was a German zen practitioner named Brigitte D'Ortschy. Although she was a first-class architect in Germany, she gave up everything, went to Japan, and once there discovered zen. She knew no Japanese and her first zen teacher, Yasutani Roshi, knew no English. But they communicated at a nonverbal level and she went at once into ever-deepening zen consciousness. A few years later, I met her at the zendo and we became great friends. I used to go over to her little one-room, thatched-roof house in Kita-Kamakura and we'd talk. Really talk. She loved a smoke now and then, so she'd insist that I join her, even though she knew I didn't smoke. Neither of us inhaled, so no great harm was done, except that the smoke would overcome even the pungent incense she often had burning.

I learned so many, many things from her. One that stands out is something that she expressed very simply: "When you come right down to it, the main thing is to quiet the mind. We must quiet our minds." At that time, I hardly understood the import of what she was saying, but now I know that if we quiet the inner dialogue of the mind, everything else will follow. It's like seeking first the reign of God, then all things will be added unto us.

Zazen is holistic. We quiet the body to influence and quiet the mind so the heart can take its natural course to the Source. This is the "heart" St. Augustine speaks of in his famous "Our hearts are made for Thee, O God, and they are restless until they rest in Thee."[2] The heart, then, is not the physical organ or the seat of emotions. It is the power by which we can experience the Infinite. Zen is totally consistent with this in strictly downgrading the ordinary intellect. Ideas and concepts are suppressed (that is, given no attention) because they are not open and are always at least one step removed from direct experience. They categorize and put things into boxes, whereas what we are seeking has no boundaries and can never be boxed in.

Although zen teachers do, of course, use the ordinary intellect and ordinary language in communicating experience and in practical instruction, nevertheless they are entirely sincere when they describe zen in the four famous phrases (of four ideograms each) that one hears again and again:
Zen is:

- A special transmission outside teaching;   (kyo-ge-betsu-den)
- Not dependent on writings;   (fu-ryu-mon-ji)

- Direct attention to a person's inner essence   (jiki-shi-nin-shin)
- Seeing one's nature and becoming a Buddha   (ken-sho-jo-butsu)

So zen is not dependent on verbal teachings and writings. Words and concepts are ultimately an obstacle. Zen is definitely right brained.

Another example of meditation with an object is to fix one's attention on the eternal questions "Who am I?" "What am I?" *Who* here refers to the Ultimate Person and *what* to the Ultimate Nature, the Source of action. But zen treats these questions very concretely: Who is sitting? What is walking? Eating? Listening? This inner questioning would seem to especially fit modern people. But even in the fourteenth century, it totally engrossed the great Japanese zen master Bassui.

Bassui

Who is the "master" within who is sitting here, who is hearing this sound? Even as a child, Bassui would often sit for hours struggling with this fundamental question, forgetful of all else. Bassui's father died when he was seven, and from that time on, this natural koan possessed him. Of a samurai family, he left to become a zen monk, but he didn't actually live at any temple. He was constantly on pilgrimage from one zen master to another, seeking help, even though he had come to many very deep insights. At each master's temple, he would stay in a hut somewhere and spend hours and hours doing zazen. Through many experiences of kensho, he came to deep realization of his True Nature. He found "The Master."

It wasn't until he was fifty years old that Bassui settled down in what is now Yamanashi Prefecture in the shadow of Mt. Fuji, the symbol of Eternal Wisdom, and accepted disciples. His temple, Kogakuji ("Facing the Mountain Temple"), grew into a great monastery of over a thousand monastic and lay students. Bassui did not write much, but what is extant of his writings is precious. They are still very popular and much used in zen circles even today. The following is an excerpt from a talk he gave. It is a vibrant, experiential description of his kind of zen that you might find helpful. It still attracts and helps me 27 years after

I first listened to Yamada Sensei's commentary on the talk in the old hall of Jomyoji.

A note before reading. Perhaps no word in Buddhist writings is more important than *Shin* (Chinese, Hsin). This Sino-Japanese ideogram is consistently translated into English as "Mind." I feel this to be a very serious mistake, because for most Westerners, mind has to do with our ordinary intellection. The basic meaning of the ideogram is *heart,* in such senses as the physical heart, the emotional center, the whole of a person's psychology, and finally, as the core or inner essence of something. All these meanings can be found in Buddhist texts, but the last is most common. It is this meaning that, in my opinion, is mistranslated as Mind. English words such as core, essence, and even "soul," are much closer to the real meaning. It is the shin of pines and cedars that the nun Ryonen asks us to listen to with our shin in her famous poem:

> Sixty-six times have these eyes beheld the changing scenes
> of autumn.
> I have said enough about moonlight. Ask me no more.
> Only listen to the voice of pines and cedars, when no wind
> stirs.[3]

I have taken the liberty of substituting the original meaning "core" whenever "mind" appears in this quotation from Bassui:

> In zazen, neither despise nor cherish the thoughts that arise; only search your own core, the very source of these thoughts. You must understand that anything appearing in your consciousness or seen by your eyes is an illusion, of no enduring reality. Hence you should neither fear nor be fascinated by such phenomena. If you keep your mind as empty as space, unstained by extraneous matters, no evil spirits can disturb you even on your deathbed. While doing zazen, however, keep none of this counsel in mind. You

must only become the question, "What is this core?" or "What is it that hears these sounds?" When you realize this core, you will know that it is the very source of all Buddhas and sentient beings. The Bodhisattva Kannon (Avalokitesvara) is so called because he attained enlightenment by perceiving (that is, grasping the source of) the sounds of the world about him.

At work, at rest, never stop trying to realize who it is that hears. Even though your questioning penetrates the unconscious, you won't find the one who hears, and all your efforts will come to naught. Yet sounds can be heard, so question yourself to an even profounder level. At last every vestige of self-awareness will disappear and you will find no "I", nor will you discover anyone who hears. This core is like the void, yet it hasn't a single spot that can be called empty. Do not mistake this state of self-realization, but continue to ask yourself even more intensely, "Now, who is it that hears?" If you bore and bore into this question, oblivious to anything else, even this feeling of voidness will vanish and you won't be aware of anything – total darkness will prevail. Don't stop here, but keep asking with all your strength, "What *is* it that hears?" Only when you have completely exhausted the questioning will the question burst; now you will feel like a man come back from the dead. This is true realization.[4]

In your meditation you may sometimes—perhaps even often—enter so deep a state that any and all words or syllables seem only to get in the way. You just become silent, but fully attentive. At such a time, you have entered into meditation without any object, without any form. The zen term for such meditation is *shikan taza*. This type of zazen is much favored by the Soto branch of Zen. Dogen Zenji, the great founder of Soto in Japan, describes shikan taza as totally alert attention that is free of thoughts, not directed to any object, void of any thought content. It is pure attention. One becomes like a satellite dish focused on Infinity. In such zazen, realization grows quickly.

Image Meditation

Finally, it would be incomplete to leave the subject of meditation without saying something about the use of imagination. We move out of zen here, because zen doesn't recommend interior imagery in meditation, although it does of course use statues and pictures for devotional practices and even petitionary prayer. I know of no Buddhist practice system that uses imagery as much and as powerfully as Vajrayana, Tibetan Buddhism. We've already seen the use of visualization in the goma ceremony of Shingon and Tendai. But both of these great sects are Tantric Buddhism, just as Vajrayana is.

Sanjusangendo is 400 ft. in length, probably the longest temple building in all Japan. In fact, it is this length that gives it its popular name, "Thirty-Three-Sections-Hall." I've been there a number of times, and it still draws me like a magnet each time I visit Kyoto. Sanjusangendo has to be long, because lined up inside on tiers are 1,001 statues of Kannon (Chinese, *Kuan Yin*), the personification of divine compassion. There is one large wooden statue of the eleven-faced, thousand-armed Kannon in the middle, flanked on either side by 500 smaller statues, all depicting this same figure of infinite mercy. The whole effect is that of an almost overwhelming expression of the unlimited compassion at work in our world.

The Tibetans represent divine compassion in both a female figure called Tara and a male figure called Chenrezi. In their pictures of the thousand-armed Chenrezi, there is an eye in each hand. With these eyes, the deity looks to the needs of each and every being and stretches out a helping hand.

A Vajrayana imagery practice is often built around Tara or Chenrezi. I'm not an expert on Tibetan meditation, though I have studied it. However, it's safe to say that such a Chenrezi meditation might go something like the following: You visualize clearly the image of the thousand-armed Chenrezi. You see the eleven faces turned in all directions, the hands and eyes full of mercy, and feel the compassion. The image is alive, vital, powerful. To begin with, Chenrezi is outside of you. Now move the image within yourself to your heart. Chenrezi disappears into the Void and there you find your True Self. Then your concrete existence begins to arise again out of the Source. This time, you rise as a Chenrezi. You, too, have eleven faces facing every-where, 1,000 eyes to see, 1,000 hands to help. They stretch out from your heart, which is filled with *bohdicitta,* the all-consuming desire and deter-mination to help all beings to the Source and the liberation of divine life. You *are* Chenrezi Bodhisattva. You *are* Kannon. With this spirit, you return to your daily life.

Is all this pure imagination, or is there some prior reality within you that you are activating through the visualization? The fact is, Kannon/Kuan Yin/Chenrezi/Tara is an archetype. I'm not thinking here of a Jungian archetype but of something even deeper—an ontological arche-type. In this case, it is the archetype of compassion and mercy. The ultimate ontological reality is the Source. This Source is pure potency, all powerful, as we say. The Source, as potency, has not any manifest form at all, but con-tains all the possible forms of existent beings prior to their ultimate mani-festation as individual beings.

The process of manifestation, or creation, is extremely complex. The point here, though, is that it begins with archetypal manifestation. Ken Wilber describes the process very well:

From the Neoplatonic traditions in the West, to the Vedanta and Mahayana and Trikaya traditions in the East, the real archetypes are *subtle seed forms upon which all of mani-festation depends.* In deep states of contemplative aware-ness, one begins to understand that the entire Kosmos emerges straight out of Emptiness, out of the primordial Purity, out of nirguna Brahman, out of the Dharmakaya, and *the first Forms* that emerge out of this Emptiness are the *basic Forms upon which all lesser forms depend for their being.* (Italics added)[5]

Just as there is a human being archetype according to which we all manifest as humans, and in which we all share, so there is the archetype of a compassionate being, in which we all share. This "subtle seed-form" of divine compassion is within each one of us waiting to be activated, to grow, and to take over our lives.

Every act of compassion ever performed anywhere, anytime, is a manifestation of this incredible force of archetypal mercy. When you see, for example, a disciple of Mother Teresa totally forget herself and give herself completely to the care of a sick person, the tears come to your eyes and you feel a powerful surge of emotion and say, "That Sister is Mercy Itself." You don't say that she is merciful but rather you use the archetypal expression *Mercy Itself.* In your perception of her, you have become aware of the archetype gloriously manifesting, so the tears come.

It is this archetypal seed-form within the practitioner that the Chenrezi meditation is devised to activate. It is meditation not so much to ask for mercy as to make us *into* Mercy. This kind of visualization releases in us all the infinite creativity of the all-powerful Source now channeled into compassion. It transforms us.

We've looked at the various Buddhist spiritual practices, especially at zazen. It's time now to go more deeply into what is being sought in all this practice. What is Buddhism looking for?

Chapter 7

SELF-DISCOVERY

The deepening stream
Becomes a silent flow
Revealing the Face.

I t is my first sesshin. We've gathered in the early evening at the Sanun Zendo. I find my assigned place and pick up the two pages of orientation. Happily, they are in English. They impressed me mightily then, some 27 years ago, and I still have them today. Besides covering many practical matters and insisting on absolute silence, the pages are very clear about the goal for this time of intense practice. We are to discover our True Face. Other terms given for the awareness we are to seek are "Buddha Nature," "True Self," or "Your Face before your parents were born."

I can still recall standing there reading these phrases, being totally intrigued by them, sensing an attraction, but feeling that I was over my head into something beyond me. At the same time, it was clear: We were there on an adventure of *self*-discovery. This is what zen is all about. It focuses solely and intently on the experience of the Self. No one has expressed the goal of Buddhist practice better than Dogen Zenji in his oft-quoted words:

> To learn the Buddha path is to learn the self.
> To learn the self is to forget the self.
> To forget the self is to experience the dropping off of mind
> and body and to perceive self as all things.
>
> (Author's translation)

Some scholars say that with the ninth-century zen master Rinzai (Chinese, Lin-Chi) there was a shift of emphasis in zen practice. For centuries, Buddhism focused on finding one's "True Nature" or "Reality," whereas Rinzai made the same search more personal—"True Self" or, to use his words, "the one True Person of no rank." Rinzai's famous koan is:

> Within this mass of reddish flesh [body]
> There is one True Person of no rank.
> This one is coming in and going out
> Of your sense organs constantly.
> If you have not yet witnessed this reality, Look! Look!
>
> Rinzairoku (Author's translation)

"Of no rank" means beyond all the categories of space, time, size, color, or form; beyond anything that the imagination or intellect could conceive. It is this Person that Rinzai himself discovered. He and all zen teachers urge us to seek till we experientially find this Self.

Who is Hearing?

I had been working on MU for four or five months and seemed to be getting nowhere. Actually, if I had gotten to no-where (or now-here), I would have been there! But what I was constantly getting was the ceaseless

chatter of my monkey mind. It was late in October and I decided to go up
to the Catholic zendo Shinmeikutsu to make my annual eight-day retreat.
It was to be in connection with my birthday.

I would be doing a lot of zazen, so in preparation I got up my
courage one evening and phoned Yamada Roshi. I asked him if I could
change my practice. I explained how things were going, and how I really felt
attracted to the *Kikunushi* koan. The whole koan is contained in the question, "*Kikunushi, nani mono zo?*" *Kiku* = to hear; *nushi* = master, the one
responsible. The rest of the phrase means "what kind of thing?" The question, then, is "Really, who/what is the one who is doing this hearing?" This,
of course, is the same as Bassui's practice described in the previous chapter.
You focus on the very act of hearing this sound in order to go to the One
who is ultimately hearing, i.e., the True Self. It is not a philosophical, intellectual question like "What is human nature?" It is an existential search.
The very kind of concrete questioning Yasutani Roshi is referring to when
he says, "The question of "Who am I?" brings you to the radiant core of your
being."[1]

Shinmeikutsu is by a river up in the mountains northwest of Tokyo.
In October it was already so damp and downright cold that I spent a good
deal of my energy battling the chill. I hardly got close to the Kikunushi at
all, but the practice I attempted there does exemplify the zen path to the
True Self.

The Evolution of Self-Consciousness

About 4,500 years ago, a definite change began in human consciousness. It didn't happen everywhere at once, and even today, there are some cultures left where the change has not yet taken place. What happened was that
humans began to be aware of themselves as separate, unique, responsible,
individual subjects. Before this, the self was primarily a group self. The individual didn't experience herself or himself as distinct from the family and
tribe. The discovery of the self as an individual subject with personal responsibility was such a great event that this kind of egocentric self-consciousness
has taken over and dominates human consciousness today.

Certainly in the West most of us live under the tyranny of ego consciousness. The light of the discovery of the ego has blinded us to the many other radiant levels of our self-reality. Above all, we have only the vaguest, hardly perceptible awareness of our Ultimate Self—the Source. So zen goes right to the jugular, to the tyranny of ego consciousness. It teaches us to forget this little local self, and to open up our awareness to the light of the Self who is the ultimately responsible One. This is what Buddhist practice is all about.

Although he may well have known nothing at all about zen, Edward Carpenter, the remarkable social scientist and poet of the late 1900s, has words which any zen master should appreciate. He truly does describe the heart of the zen path. I've added some italics to encourage your deeper consideration.

> If you *inhibit thought* (and persevere) you come at length to a region of consciousness below or *behind thought* ... and to a realization of an altogether *vaster self* than that to which we are accustomed. And since the *ordinary consciousness* with which we are concerned in ordinary life is before all things *founded on the little local self* ... it follows that to pass out of that is to die to the ordinary self and the ordinary world.

> It is to die in the ordinary sense, but in another, it is to wake up and find that the "I", *one's real, most intimate self, pervades the universe* and all other things. So great, so splendid, is this experience, that it may be said that all minor questions and doubts fall away in the face of it; and certain it is that in thousands and thousands of cases, the fact of its having come even once to an individual has completely revolutionized his subsequent life and outlook on the world.[2]

The Ten Ox Pictures

Daitokuji is a large complex of temples and gardens in northern Kyoto. Like so many other people, I deeply love Kyoto, and for me Daitokuji is one of its special places. There is even a sub-temple, Zuihoin, which was built by Otomo Sorin, a feudal lord from Kyushu who was converted to Christianity by Francis Xavier. One of its gardens features some rocks artfully arranged as a cross. But it wasn't at Zuihoin that I saw the ten ox pictures. It was in another sub-temple whose name I have forgotten. The temple wasn't usually open to the public, but a friend arranged for me to visit it.

The temple attendant showed us into one large room where I was happy to see all ten ox pictures depicted on the sliding doors which served as walls on three sides. As I admired the now-faded paintings, I noticed that they were out of order! This in spite of the fact that each picture had its own number clearly written. What should I do? It might embarrass the attendant if I pointed out the mistake. But, perfectionist that I am, I couldn't just let them be. So I pretended that I didn't know much about the pictures, and simply pointed out that according to the numbers, they seemed out of order. I've forgotten what happened then, but I do know that these pictures have impressed me more and more as the years go by.

The ten ox pictures are a graphic presentation of the zen path to the experience of the True Self. There are a number of different series depicting in a linear way the zen development process. One series has only six pictures, another eight. Recently, during a trip to China, we drove out from Chunching to Dazu where there are whole hillsides covered with ancient Buddhist carvings. The carvings we saw were done in the ninth century. Sure enough, there was a series of carvings of our old friend the ox. They were weather-beaten, and some were indistinct, but it seemed to be a series of eight. The set of pictures that is most popular in Japan and the one I'm most familiar with is a set of ten with both a prose and a poetic commentary, all done by the twelfth-century Chinese master Kakuan (Chinese, Kuo-an).

Probably because of the sacred character of the ox in India, this animal came to symbolize the primal nature of reality, our True Self. The pictures show the developmental advance in human consciousness culminating in the definitive, integrating experience of the Self. The process is depicted in a linear way, but in reality, no one goes in perfect succession from one stage to the next, up to the perfect zen person of picture ten. We advance a stage or two, and then fall back. We dip into a higher consciousness, and then backslide into a lower. It is helpful, though, to take them in order.

The pictures, and therefore the path, can be divided into three sections. Rather than go into a detailed explanation of the first two sections, I'd prefer to give little more than the titles of each picture. Section one has three stages:

Picture 1:   "Seeking the Ox" (Who am I? / What am I?)

Picture 2:   "Finding the Traces" (of the True Self in the lives and writings of enlightened people)

Picture 3:   "First Glimpse of the Ox"
This is kensho, the first experience of the Self. It can be of varying degrees.)

Except for the moment of kensho, and perhaps shortly after, at this third stage the seeker is still dominated by the discriminating intellect and the dualistic consciousness, There is still the subject self, I, seeking the object Self, Me.

The second section is a process of gradual integration. The dualism between "I" (subject) seeking the True Self (object) progressively diminishes. The very titles show how the person is coming closer to the ox (Self):

Picture 4:   "Catching the Ox"

Picture 5:   "Taming the Ox"

Picture 6:   "Riding the Ox Home"

Picture 7:   "Ox Forgotten, Self Alone"

This section culminates in number seven, in which the ox, which was only a skillful means for use in our dualistic state of consciousness, disappears. Ordinary subject/object cognition is quieted. But some sense of *self* remains.

The third section presents zen perfection. Pictures eight through ten describe a remarkable series of awareness states. They depict *what* one discovers at the climax of the zen search and teach what the True Self is.

Picture 8:   "Both Ox and Self Forgotten"

Picture 9:   "Returning to the Source"

Picture 10:   "Entering the Marketplace with Bliss
                Bestowing Hands"

These captions clearly describe the enlightenment of Yamada Roshi, my zen master.

Chapter 8

THE EMPTY-FULL SELF

Out of the Empty Sky
Mountains, rivers, galaxies
And laughing joy.

In late November of 1953, not even three months after I arrived in Japan and hardly ten miles from where I was living, an event took place that would have a deep influence on my life and on the lives of many thousands all around the globe. Yamada Kozo, a Japanese business executive, had a profound zen experience. This man, of course, was to become our Yamada Roshi. He writes about his experience in a letter to his old friend Nakagawa Soen Roshi.

Who Am I? What Am I? — The Answer

The account is so richly instructive and inspiring, I'll quote it at length (The full account is contained in Philip Kapleau's *The Three Pillars of Zen*.). I have again substituted "core" for "mind."

The day after I called on you [Nakagawa] I was riding home on the train with my wife. I was reading a book on Zen by Son-o, who, you may recall, was a master of Soto Zen living in Sendai during the Genroku period [1688-1703]. As the train was nearing Ofuna station I ran across this line: "I came to realize clearly that core is no other than mountains and rivers and the great wide earth, the sun and the moon and the stars."

I had read this before, but this time it impressed itself upon me so vividly that I was startled. I said to myself: "After seven or eight years of zazen I have finally perceived the essence of this statement," and couldn't suppress the tears that began to well up. Somewhat ashamed to find myself crying among the crowd, I averted my face and dabbed at my eyes with my handkerchief.

Meanwhile the train had arrived at Kamakura station and my wife and I got off. On the way home I said to her: "In my present exhilarated frame of mind I could rise to the greatest heights." Laughingly she replied: "Then where would I be?" All the while I kept repeating that quotation to myself.

It so happened that that day my younger brother and his wife were staying at my home, and I told them about my visit to your monastery and about the American [Philip Kapleau] who had come to Japan again only to attain enlightenment. In short, I told them all the stories you told me, and it was after eleven thirty before I went to bed.

At midnight I abruptly awakened. At first my mind was foggy, then suddenly that quotation flashed into my consciousness: "I came to realize clearly that core is no other than mountains, rivers, and the great wide earth, the sun and the moon and the stars." And I repeated it. Then all at once I was struck as though by lightning, and the next instant heaven and earth crumbled and disappeared. Instantaneously, like surging waves, a tremendous delight welled up in me, a veritable hurricane of delight, as I laughed loudly and wildly: "Ha, ha, ha, ha, ha, ha! There's no reasoning here, no reasoning at all! Ha, ha, ha!" The empty sky split in two, then opened its enormous mouth and began to laugh uproariously: "Ha, ha, ha!" Later one of the members of my family told me that my laughter had sounded inhuman...

"I've come to enlightenment! Shakyamuni and the patriarchs haven't deceived me! They haven't deceived me!" I remember crying out. When I calmed down I apologized to the rest of the family, who had come downstairs frightened by the commotion.

Prostrating myself before the photograph of Kannon you had given me, the Diamond sutra, and my volume of the book written by Yasutani-roshi, I lit a stick of incense and did zazen until it was consumed half an hour later, though it seemed only two or three minutes had elapsed.

Even now my skin is quivering as I write.

That morning I went to see Yasutani-roshi and tried to describe to him my experience of the sudden disintegration of heaven and earth. "I am overjoyed, I am overjoyed!" I kept repeating, striking my thigh with vigor. Tears came which I couldn't stop. I tried to relate to him the experience of that night, but my mouth trembled and words wouldn't

form themselves. In the end I just put my face in his lap.
Patting me on the back he said: "Well, well, it is rare indeed
to experience to such a wonderful degree. It is termed
'Attainment of the emptiness of core.' You are to be con-
gratulated!"

"Thanks to you," I murmured, and again wept for joy.
Repeatedly I told him: "I must continue to apply myself
energetically to zazen." He was kind enough to give me
detailed advice on how to pursue my practice in the future,
after which he again whispered in my ear, "My congratula-
tions!" and escorted me to the foot of the mountain by
flashlight. [1]

There are a host of rich insights to be garnered from this account,
but let's go to the very heart of the event as expressed in the words of
Yamada Roshi himself. When he went to see Yasutani Roshi early in the
morning, he says, "I tried to describe to him my experience of the sudden
disintegration of heaven and earth." The earlier description he gives is
"…the next instant *heaven and earth crumbled and disappeared.*" He finally calls what he is experiencing an *"empty sky."* His consciousness has pen-
etrated to the absolute core (shin) of himself and of all things. What he discovers there is Emptiness! The disintegration of heaven and earth means
that all distinctions, all categories of being, all means of identifying anything have disappeared. Yasutani Roshi declares the breakthrough as the
"Attainment of the emptiness of core." As the Core of his own self and of all
things, Yamada has directly experienced a No-thing-ness, a Void. The
ideogram for void or emptiness is the same for sky. Throughout all of
Buddhism, the empty sky is the most common symbol for the pure emptiness at the heart of all reality.

Notice the circumstances of Yamada Roshi's experience. First, his
consciousness was filled with Son-o's words about the Ultimate. Secondly,
it happened just as he awoke. There are two very precious times when true

awareness can arise—when we are either just falling asleep or just waking. This is because at such times our ordinary discriminating consciousness and egocentric thinking are not yet up to full strength. These moments are chinks in the armor of the dualistic, egocentric consciousness. They are openings to the infinite. Also, isn't it interesting that it happened at midnight, at the zero hour? This was most appropriate, because the Roshi's enlightenment began with the eighth ox picture, which is a large zero.

So besides the sky, the other great symbol for that which is at the heart of everything is a zero, a circle (in Japanese, *enso*). In nearly all of the renditions of the ox path, every picture is enclosed in this zero. We can talk about *what* is encompassed inside the circle, but the zero, shin itself is the foundation. The circle is a symbol of the core of reality. It is indescribable, ineffable, beyond all words or images, without boundaries of time or space, outside all distinctions of right/wrong, true/false, beautiful/ugly. It was because of this same experience that the Buddha, when asked about the Ultimate, kept, as they say, a "noble silence." He said nothing about no-thing.

Also to be noted is the Roshi's cry, "There's no reasoning here, no reasoning at all!" As you can already see, this is totally consonant with that which he had discovered. All our usual modes of perceiving, conceptualizing, and reasoning have to do with distinguishing things and putting them into categories. Such mind work cannot possibly take us to that which is beyond all categories. These usual modes of perception were eclipsed by another power, that by which we experience the infinite. The activation of this power of perception happened that night because of the thousands of hours of zazen in which he had quieted his mind. There was also the happy circumstance of his just waking.

There in his house, near the foot of the Kamakura Daibutsu, Yamada Kozo joined Shakyamuni Buddha in the experience of the Ultimate Core of reality. Even at the time, he clearly knew this: "I've come to enlightenment! Shakyamuni and the patriarchs haven't deceived me! They haven't deceived me!" As Kapleau points out, this expression is a traditional way of declaring that the enlightenment transmitted by Shakyamuni and the Buddhist patriarchs is now one's own existential experience.

"Instantaneously, like surging waves, a tremendous delight welled up in me, a veritable hurricane of delight, as I laughed loudly and wildly: 'Ha, ha, ha, ha, ha, ha!'...I am overjoyed, I am overjoyed!" What on earth is so joyful about discovering *no thing*? What tremendous delight is there in entering *emptiness*? Why laugh uproariously at the *disintegration* of heaven and earth? The root of all this joy is found in the fact that this discovery of the Void is not a negative but a profoundly positive experience. Together with the discovery comes the "Return to the Source," which is the title of the ninth ox picture. Built into finding the Void is the encounter with it as pure potency. It is all-power-full. Emptiness is seen to be full of everything that can possibly exist, not as existing but as potential. Kapleau describes this as follows:

> Questioner: What is Buddhist emptiness? I know what the books say: It's the void, *sunyata,* and all that. But what is meant by "Form is only emptiness, emptiness only form?" [Kapleau] Roshi: Suppose you are a craftsman working in silver, and you want to make a small figure of a buddha. When your silver is molten and flowing, it has the possibility of actualizing itself into any object – that's emptiness, no-thingness. Then you pour the molten metal into the mold and it hardens – that's form. But now let us say that after you have formed your buddha you are dissatisfied with it and wish to make something else with the same silver. So you melt down the figure, and the silver returns to formlessness. In essence, then, this emptiness is no different from the form.[2]

The experience of the Source as source and what this means is not spelled out in the original description of Yamada's enlightenment. As the integration of his experience into his whole psychology continued over the next few days, he expresses in his diary much more clearly his return to the void as Source.

Am totally at peace at peace…

Am supremely free free free free free…

There is no common man.

The big clock chimes—not the clock but shin chimes. The universe itself chimes. There is neither shin nor universe. Dong, dong, dong!

I've totally disappeared. Buddha is!…

Oh, you *are!* You laughed didn't you? This laughter is the sound of your plunging into the world…

Ding, dong! The clock chimed. This alone *is!* This alone *is!* There is no reasoning here.

Surely the world has changed [with awakening]. But in what way?

The ancients said the enlightened mind is comparable to a fish swimming.

That's exactly how it is—there's no stagnation. I feel no hindrance.

Everything flows smoothly, freely. Everything goes naturally. This limitless freedom is beyond all expression. What a wonderful world![3]

Consider the Roshi's statements. "The big clock chimes—not the clock but core chimes." In the middle of the night, he hears the clock in his house. In his very hearing of the chimes, he finds that the Void is making the chiming sound. It is the Source of all sound. The Void is the One who is responsible for the existence of any and all things. He has found the One who is hearing, the One who is chiming, the One responsible for the Many (all of creation). He is this One. This is why he says, "I've totally disappeared. Buddha is!" He realizes that his little ego-self is not the ultimate hearer of the chimes, his True Self is. He, in his Buddha nature, is the One acting in all activity in the whole universe. He knows that every one of us at root is this True Self. So he says, "There is no common man." We are all glorious Buddhas! This is the true human self-identification, even though most of us hardly realize it.

The Source is intelligent and responsible for all action everywhere in the universe. In this sense, it must be thought of as personal. Not a limited, human person, but the all-embracing, divine person manifesting as individual persons. And again, each one of us is identical with this Source. We are, each of us, the "one True Person of no rank" that Master Rinzai speaks of. It is our oneness in the one True Person that is the reason for all the Roshi's immense joy. No doubt, he had been struggling through his eight years of zen. This struggle is basically over, so this is why he says, "Am totally at peace at peace." But *joy* arises out of oneness and love. He is now concretely experiencing the One Source doing everything. This dynamic oneness takes over his consciousness. "Ding, dong! The clock chimed. This alone is! This alone is!" There is only One that is–es, and we—each and every doer at any level of being, all creatures great and small—are that One.

His expression "The universe itself chimes," will be taken up in the next chapter. Also, don't be disturbed by his saying, "There is neither core nor universe." Those thoughts are abstractions and don't exist like the Ultimate in this "Dong, dong, dong!"

What Yamada says about his laughter is absolutely fascinating. It is pure insight. "Oh, you are! You laughed, didn't you? The laughter is the sound of your plunging into the world." First, he discovers the Formless Void and realizes that *this* is what he is. Then he experiences this Formlessness as the Source of all forms, of all existent being in the world.

Heaven and earth crumbled and disappeared. Now it all rises again and he is plunged back into this world. He himself is-es in it all. "What a wonderful world!" In pure joy, he laughs, ha, ha, ha!

The world is wonderful, not just because of its oneness, but also because of its dynamic freedom. "Surely the world has changed. But in what way?°I feel no hindrance. Everything flows smoothly, freely." The movement of the Formless Source into the form of chiming clock and burning incense is a totally free movement. At the level of perception that the Roshi is at now, all this action is seen in its intrinsic purity. His whole psychology is pure and all his processes of perception can take in this intrinsic purity. They are uninhibited by the obstructions of egocentric consciousness. There are no judgments of like or dislike, right or wrong. No rejection or attachment. All is seen according to its ultimate and true nature. "Everything goes naturally." And since he is aware of his own be-ing as the movement of the Source, he joyfully cries, "Am supremely free free free free."

Chapter 9

THE BODHISATTVA PATH

The empty Stream
Is full to overflowing
In boundless compassion.

Another expression that can be used to describe the ten ox pictures is the Bodhisattva Path. The literal meaning of the Sanskrit word *bodhisattva* is something like "enlightenment being." This indicates a person of the highest insight and wisdom. But the distinguishing characteristic of such a being is the compassion which moves the person to continue working in our world until all beings are saved.

Transcendent and Earthly Bodhisattvas

Mahayana Buddhism distinguishes two types of bodhisattvas: transcendent and earthly. The former are the great universal beings like Kannon, the special personification of merciful compassion, and Monju (Sanskrit, Manjushri), the one whose wisdom dispels the darkness of ignorance. The only image allowed in a traditional zendo is that of Monju Bosatsu. (*Bosatsu* is bodhisattva in Japanese.) These transcendental bodhisattvas are archetypes, not historical beings. However, they do enter history in their striking incarnations which arise now and then. Kannon, for example, is present in every act of merciful compassion that any person does in any age.

An earthly bodhisattva or bosatsu is an historical person who is distinguished by wisdom, compassion, and a powerful determination to assist others. Yamada Roshi was certainly such a person. He did have defects which showed up at times, but especially after his great experience, he was truly a bodhisattva for the many, many people from all over the world that he influenced.

1. He definitively discovered the True Self.
2. In this experience he found that he was one with all people, all reality.
3. He saw the blindness and suffering of people.
4. He gave himself up to helping people to enlightenment.
5. He persevered in this as long as his life on this earth lasted and, we can be sure, continues this same work in his new state of life.

The truth of the matter is that, by our very nature, we are all called to this same ideal. Let us see in more detail how the path proceeds.

Ox Pictures 8 and 9

The ox path is a consciousness adventure. In Chapter 7, we saw that the first seven ox pictures all lead up to the third section, stages 8 through 10. The eighth or "zero" stage is sometimes called the Great Cessation or the Great Death. The return to and self-identification with the Void is clearly a death—not a physical death, but a psychological death. At #8, a person consciously dies (albeit not physically). One's own self crumbles and disappears along with the disintegration of heaven and earth. But this death is not annihilation.

The next step is again an awareness event. In #9, the Return to the Source, the Formless Void is seen as pure potency out of which one's self and all beings arise. Having undergone disintegration, the self and all reality rise in resurrection. It was this experience of the whole universe arising out of the Source that Yamada Roshi called his "plunging into the world."

In the final stage, the tenth picture, the risen person returns as a bodhisattva to the world, filled with compassion and a great drive to help all. But before looking more closely at this final stage, we must see what returning to the Source does to a person's self-identity.

I was down at Fuji Seishin, the school and residence of the Religious of the Sacred Heart, in Susono at the foot of Mt. Fuji. Fuji Seishin is located in Shizuoka, which is certainly one of the most beautiful of all the prefectures in Japan. Its crowning beauty is Mt. Fuji. I remember taking the opportunity to visit Ryutakuji, which was close by. This was the temple of Yamada Roshi's great friend Nakagawa Soen Roshi. It is a Rinzai Zen temple founded by Hakuin Zenji, one of the greatest mystics of Japan.

I asked if I could see Soen Roshi and was shown into the parlor. This was, of course, a Japanese-style room and had the usual *tokonoma*. A tokonoma is an alcove in the best room of a house and is the spiritual and cultural center of the home. I was looking at an old scroll hanging in the tokonoma when Sasaki Sensei came in to tell me that Soen Roshi was ill and could not receive visitors. Partly out of the expected politeness, but also because I was genuinely curious, I admired the tokonoma and asked him to read for me the ideograms beautifully written on the scroll. He obliged, saying, "Kenkon itaru tokoro waga, ie."

At the time, that made hardly more sense to me than it does, perhaps, to you who are now reading these words. I copied them down in a little notebook. Of course, he tried to explain their meaning, but I still didn't really understand. My life in Japan was mostly like living in a verbal fog. This, too, was an unexpected part of the training to get me out of my head. However, one thing was clear. This was one of the temple's treasures, because, as Sasaki Sensei told me, it was written for Hakuin by his own zen teacher, Shoju Rojin, and Hakuin had left it in this monastery.

When I returned to the language school, I finally found *kenkon* in the dictionary. It is a somewhat poetic way of saying heaven (ken) and earth (kon). So a rather literal translation of the scroll is, "My home extends to heaven and earth." Even then, the inner meaning of the phrase was beyond me. However, as I entered more and more into the zen mind-set, I came to understand it as an expression of the basic truth that in the discovery of your Buddha nature, you find that you are truly one with everybody and everything. Your self-identity, your "I," now extends to heaven and earth. Everywhere is your home.

One of the classic stories of Buddhism is that of the baby Siddhartha, Shakyamuni Buddha, standing up and declaring, "In the whole universe, I alone exist!" Reflect for a moment what kind of "I" is revealed in this sentence. What kind of self-identity is being expressed?

Why does discovery of the Source reveal that each of us is one with everything? Why does this experience so change our self-identification that the "I" of each one now extends to the universe? When I see a tree, why do I have to say, "There am I!"? Why does enlightenment move us from a self-awareness that excludes everyone else ("I am not you") to one that includes everyone ("I am you")? The reason is that the Source cannot be divided. In the Formless Void, there is no thing to divide. The Source is totally present in every manifestation. The All-Mighty is holographically present at all times in every existent being. (*holos* = whole; *graph* = written. The whole is written in every part.) As a consequence, we can say philosophically: You are one with the Source. Ultimately, you *are* the Source. Therefore, wherever the Source is manifesting, you are. I have spelled this out in a logical way, but in his experience, Yamada Roshi discovered it *directly*. As he said, crying out, "There's no reasoning here! No reasoning at all!"

Hakuin Zenji was at the end of a sesshin at a temple across the mountains from Tokyo. He had probably stayed up all night doing zazen. The great bell rang out in the early morning silence, calling the monks to the recitation of the sutras. From a distance, Hakuin heard the bell and shouted out, "Hey, I just rang!" His "I," which is The Source manifesting, is acting everywhere.

A very good friend, Fr. William Johnston, S.J., felt this same kind of self-identity even in the successor to the great Harada Daiun Roshi (Yasutani Roshi's teacher). After Fr. Johnston returned from a sesshin under this roshi, also called Harada, I phoned him at Sophia University in Tokyo to ask him how things went. He spoke about the cold he had had and told of his dokusan with the Roshi. Then I asked him how Harada was. I've never forgotten his response: "Harada Roshi, there's a man who is the universe."

As zen moves into mainstream America, this fundamental Buddhist insight is coming to be expressed even in jokes. For example, a zen monk goes up to a hot dog vendor outside an amusement park and places his order: "Make me one with everything."

There is the story of the California businessman from Marin County who went to Korea for the first time. He was into things Eastern and was looking forward to his first trip to the Orient. When he came out of the gate at Kempo Airport in Seoul, a well-dressed Korean man came up to him, bowed, and said what sounded like, "I am you." "Golly," the Marin man thought, "my first step in the Orient and I encounter the very essence of Eastern wisdom!" The man then gave him his business card. On it, in both Korean and English, was his name: Chulsu Yu. Nevertheless, what the Californian heard was true.

Another story is about the Dalai Lama's birthday. His monks gave him a huge box, nicely wrapped. When he unwrapped it, he looked inside and cried out, "Oh! Just what I've always wanted—nothing!"

A zen sesshin was not an easy thing for me. There were lots of pains, but worst of all were mealtimes. I had no trouble with the silence. I actually enjoyed the blows of the *kyosaku*, the stick the Roshi's assistant would hit people's shoulders with to help them in the sitting. The reduced sleep wasn't all that bad, except when we stayed up all night on the eve of December eighth. But my legs were a different thing, especially my knees. They hurt. The rhythm of the zazen was 25-minute periods of sitting interspersed with about 10 minutes of walking *kinhin* (meditation). By alternating one period of sitting on the cushion with one on a little meditation bench, I managed fairly well. The pain wouldn't get *too* bad. But the meals went on much longer than 25 minutes. I loved the food, but the pain in my knees could get so excruciating that enjoying it was terribly difficult. The reason the meals took so long was because every detail of the meal was a ritual that had to be performed with great reverence. It was a practice of that reverence an enlightened person has toward everything, even though many of us had little enlightenment. Every grain of rice had to be eaten with thanksgiving and reverence, because *the whole universe is in each grain of rice*!

What on earth does that mean? Each time I heard it, I felt something, but didn't understand at all. The same insight is found in Yamada Roshi's "The universe itself chimes." Such statements are simply a further development of the insight of Self discovery. Recall again that the Source is present in every manifestation, even in a tiny rice grain. But the whole universe is really (albeit potentially) present in the Source. Nothing ever leaves the Source. So wherever the Source is, there is the universe!

There is one final step to the unpacking of a deep zen *satori* or enlightenment experience. The world is *dynamic*. It is moving, changing, evolving. Notice how Yamada says, "Everything *flows* smoothly, freely. Everything goes naturally." This flow is the movement of the Formless Source into form manifestation. It is also the movement of manifestation back to the Source, in order to move (rise) into new form. So we find three basic constituents of reality: the Source, the Form, and the Movement.

Here it is extremely important to realize that these are not three beings. The Source alone is not an existent being. A form manifestation alone is not an existent being. Nor is the Movement. The three together constitute a being. You could describe them as components. To "exist" is an interesting verb. It means to stand (sta) out (ex). The *form manifestation stands out* from the pure undifferentiated *Source*. To exist demands all three components italicized in this last sentence. *Every being is a Dynamic Formless/Form reality.*

I'd ask you to keep these ideas about "Formless/Form Movement" in mind, because when we return to Christianity, they will enter into our understanding of the Christ-life and of the Trinity.

Ox Picture 10

After his zero hour experience, Yamada Roshi continued his practice. As he said that morning to Yasutani Roshi, "I must continue to apply myself energetically to zazen." When I met him some 15 years later, he was already established as Yasutani's main successor and had largely taken over the direction of the Kamakura zen group. Because so little of it is available, property in Japan is exceedingly precious. Yet Yamada Roshi took the whole section behind his house, and with his own money built the Sanun Zendo. His intention was to assist not just Japanese but also foreigners on the path to enlightenment.

With the beautiful cooperation of his wife, the zendo flourished. The Roshi and Miyazaki Sensei welcomed people of various religions from many countries, with a largeness of heart that was extraordinary. They would help people with visa problems and do anything they could to ease their stay in Japan. The Roshi spent thousands upon thousands of hours in dokusan, in preparing and giving *teisho* (formal zen talks), in writing a book on koans and many other articles, and in directing the organization of the whole zen group, which is called Sanbo Kyodan. As his students spread around the world, the Roshi went to them in Hawaii and the U.S. mainland, to the Philippines, and to Europe. The sesshin he directed at the Bishop's house in Leyte, Philippines, was described as a kind of Pentecost because so many came to kensho. All these activities went on year after year for over 25 years until Yamada Roshi's death in 1989.

When we reflect on all this, we must say that he was clearly a modern bodhisattva. Even this book, such as it is, is an extension of his light and compassion. Yamada Koun Roshi truly did "enter the marketplace [of human relationships and human strivings] with bliss-bestowing hands." The last words of the poetic commentary on the tenth picture certainly fit his life's work:

> "Without recourse to mystic powers,
> Withered trees he swiftly brings to bloom."

The Bodhisattva Path

No one has written with more depth and beauty about the bodhisattva ideal than the Indian scholar-saint Shantideva of the seventh/eighth centuries. The following is a lengthy quotation from his *Guide to the Bodhisattva Way of Life*, beautifully translated by Stephen Batchelor.

Thus by the virtue collected
Through all that I have done,
May the pain of every living creature
Be completely cleared away!

May I be the doctor and the medicine
And may I be the nurse
For all sick beings in the world
Until everyone is healed.

May a rain of food and drink descend
To clear away the pain of thirst and hunger,
And during the eon of famine
May I myself change into food and drink!

May I become an inexhaustible treasure
For those who are poor and destitute;
May I turn into all the things they need
And may these be placed close beside them!

Without any sense of loss
I shall give up my body and enjoyments,
As well as my virtues of past, present, future,
For the sake of benefiting all!

By giving up all, sorrow is transcended
And my mind will realize the sorrowless state.
It is best that I now give everything to all beings
In the same way as I shall at death!

Having given this body up
For the pleasure of all living beings,
By killing, abusing, and beating it,
May they always do as they please!

Although they may play with my body,
And make it a source of jest and blame,
Because I have given it up to them,
What is the use of holding it dear?

Therefore I shall let them do anything to it,
As long as it does not cause them harm,
And whenever anyone encounters me,
May it never be meaningless for him!

Whether those who encounter me
Conceive a faithful or any angry thought,
May that always become the source
For fulfilling all their wishes!

May all who say bad things to me
Or cause me any harm,
And those who mock and insult me
Have the fortune to awaken fully!

May I be Savior of those without one,
A guide for all travelers on the way;
May I be a bridge, a boat, and a ship,
For all who wish to cross the water!

May I be an island for those who seek one,
And a lamp for those desiring light!
May I be a bed for all who wish to rest,
And a slave for all who want a slave!

May I be a wishing jewel, a magic vase,
Powerful mantras, and great medicine,
May I become a wish-fulfilling tree,
And a cow of plenty for the world!

Just like space
And the great elements such as earth,
May I always support the life
Of all the countless creatures! [1]

Chapter 10

A MARGINAL MAN

Here at the margin
The dawning light reveals
I'm at the Center.

One afternoon, I went for a little hike with Tom Charbeneau, S.J., in the hills behind our Jesuit high school in Hiroshima. It was probably around 1964. Tom was into sociology. That might have been the background for a remark he made as we hiked and talked, a remark that so impressed me that it became a part of me: "We are marginal men." Ever since that day, this is how I describe myself. "I'm a marginal man."

In spite of my deep and abiding love for Japan, its people, and its culture, I'm still marginal there. So much of the culture, the language, the mind-set, and even to some degree the social relations are more or less inaccessible to me. In spite of a powerful feeling of affinity and respect for everyone and everything Japanese, I must also admit my marginality. But I also feel I'm on the margin of American culture. There is so much that I do and so much that I don't resonate with in this country. To some degree, the same must be said of my status in the Society of Jesus. Even as a Jesuit, I feel quite marginal a good deal of the time. Finally, the same must be said about the zendo. I was there, but never felt I was fully there.

The Jesuit residence at the Hiroshima Gakuin is built on a hillside. Below is the ball field and to its right the narrow road leading up to the school. I don't know how many times during my last year or two of teaching at the Gakuin I stood at my third-floor window and said, as I saw the students playing and perhaps a parent or two coming up the road, "This isn't me." Finally, I asked myself, "Where do I feel at home? What work would feel right for me?" I realized that whenever I directed a summer retreat I would invariably stand up, look out the window of whatever room I was staying in, and say—even out loud—"This is me." Now as I reflect, it must have again been that single-minded interest in God and the spiritual path that was asserting itself at both windows. I was marginal to everything else.

Finally, the time came for me to move on. I was on a train from Hiroshima to Tokyo. A small crowd had seen me off at the station, because after eight years of teaching at the Gakuin I was leaving to become the spiritual director of the Jesuit language school near Tokyo. Seated there by myself in the train, with my back to Hiroshima, I had an almost eerie experience. It was as if I had a book in my hands, the book of my life. There, on that train, I came to the last page of the "Gakuin" chapter. It was just as if I calmly turned the page to begin the new chapter. And I have never turned back to that Gakuin chapter. Everyone said I'd done a good job during my years there. I had no regrets. But a lot of the time, I hadn't fully been there.

I am still marginal. In fact, I cannot remember a departure from any place at which I was so deeply affected that I really didn't want to leave. What does this say about me? In some sense, I am "a free and easy wanderer," but certainly not in the full sense of the Taoist ideal those words describe.

There must be many factors coming together to make me so marginal. Certainly I am an introvert. And my slow awakening into consciousness played a big part. But why am I not really aware and committed? I'd say that it has been all rooted in the fact that I can't forget my self. The little local self looks *at* everything and doesn't become one *with* anything. When there is no oneness, there is no real love. Breaking away from a relationship in which there is no depth of love causes little pain. Self-consciousness keeps us always marginal.

On the other hand, as my statements standing at the two windows show, I think that perhaps my marginality also arises to some extent from my interest in God and the spiritual path. I acknowledge the danger of becoming a kind of spiritual snob, but so many parts of our culture, even the arts and the politics of religion, are not my abiding interest. So I end up being marginal to them.

This detachment holds sway not only in regard to places and social situations, but also in the field of mental paradigms. Brought up and fully trained in I still feel marginal even to them. I'd been practicing zen for two or three years when I was talking one evening with Bob Rush, S.J., in the recreation room of the Kamakura language school. Suddenly I said, "My loyalty to Christ is no longer determined by my observance of canon law." When I said this, I realized that something had been changing within me. I still observe Church law, but deep down it has no hold on me. There's freedom and no fear. It's definitely on the margin of my life.

A year or two after that, I recall saying to a Jesuit seminarian that my loyalty to Christ no longer demanded rigid loyalty to Church dogma. Furthermore, one time when I was walking in the meager garden in front of the language school, I felt a freedom well up within me regarding the institutional Church itself. I really felt I didn't *have* to be a Catholic, while at the same time, my commitment to Christ remained as strong as ever. In fact, my appreciation of the Church continues to grow, but I am not in it like most people think I am.

I left the zendo after only six years of formal training. There were no external reasons why I couldn't continue on. I didn't move away from Kamakura. I wasn't too busy to attend the zazenkai and sesshin. I've never written about why I left the training and rarely talk about it. As I reflect now, I can say that it was because *I still felt too marginal to advanced consciousness.*

Kensho and Leaving the Zendo

I had been trying my best with breathing awareness, with MU, with Kikunushi, and even at times with shikan taza. I knew that my consciousness was changing, but I just couldn't seem to break through to kensho. I'd had a lot of lights and insights. One time during a summer sesshin at Takatsuki near Osaka, while walking on the roof at night, I somehow felt truly one with the stars, but my reflective intellect at once moved back onto front stage in my psyche, and the moment passed. Then, there was the July morning at Higashimurayama outside Tokyo during a weekend of charismatic prayer with five other foreigners. I woke up very early. While I was lying there, some words of Yasutani Roshi came into my mind. "There is a world beyond good and evil. You must go beyond all distinctions like right/wrong, like/dislike, beautiful/ugly, good/evil." Suddenly, I felt a shift inside, and I knew that he was right. I *knew* that world beyond good and evil. I mentioned this to the others when we met for prayer later in the morning, but aside from Fr. Bill Johnston, no one seemed to have any idea of what I was talking about. Nevertheless, ever since then, the problem of evil doesn't bother me. Down deep, I know it's all alright.

During a sesshin at Takatsuki near Osaka, I was in such a state of meditation that the napkin at lunchtime was luminous and each bodily movement seemed outlined in flashing light. But at once, I reflected that all this was really nothing more than an indication that I was in a sensitive state.

It was during that sesshin that I went into dokusan and Yamada Roshi asked me to show him MU. I did so very simply. He questioned me further and I responded at once. "That is fine," he said. "I affirm your kensho." He followed this with instructions on how to proceed in zazen. I didn't know what to do. Could this be the kensho I had been hoping for all these years? I certainly was in a fine meditative state, but I felt I had answered his questions too much from my head. There was no exaltation of spirit. No sense of an awakening breakthrough.

I admit I was relieved to finally move on from MU, but at the same time disappointed and even a bit disillusioned. There is a simple ceremony at the end of each sesshin in which the Roshi asks any and all who have come to kensho since the last sesshin to go around to each person in attendance and make a *gassho* of gratitude (a bow with hands together). I definitely felt grateful to each person there, but at the same time, I felt somewhat like a fake.

I began going through the koans, but every time I was puzzled by something, I felt that this was because I really had no kensho. Given my history of low self-esteem, you can imagine my inner conflict. Even at Takatsuki, the Roshi had seen my confusion and had assured me to go ahead. He told me that kensho doesn't always have to be a big emotional experience, that it can be simple and quiet. But the suspicion remained. Hadn't he just been kind and passed me through the "gateless barrier" of MU? (Gateless Barrier is the title of the *Mumonkan*, the koan collection which begins with the MU koan.)

This insecurity and sense of insincerity gnawed away inside me. At last, I could stand it no more. After six or seven months of koan work, I told the Roshi that I felt it would be best for my progress on the path if I would temporarily suspend formal zen practice for a while. His response was so big and compassionate. He never held anyone to himself. He immediately said something like, "That is fine. In the matter of your path, you must do what you deeply feel is best." I am sorry that I never returned.

Now, over twenty years later, I can't help but feel that both of us were right. I was definitely only on the thin margin of the world of advanced consciousness. My dualistic mind was still strong. I surely had one foot and a good part of the other in the dualistic world of ego consciousness. I was still very small-self-conscious. But the Roshi was also quite correct. My awareness had definitely been shifting. In his keen discernment, he saw this margin on the enlightened world. He saw more deeply into me than I could see into myself at that time.

Gradual Enlightenment

There are two schools in zen regarding enlightenment, the sudden and the gradual enlightenment schools. In general, Soto Zen favors the gradual, Rinzai the sudden. The Sambo Kyodan, which has roots in both Soto and Rinzai practices, seems to favor the sudden, but acknowledges the gradual. Sudden enlightenment happens in very perceptible experiences that clearly lift a person up to new levels of awareness. Usually it is preceded by a period of buildup and tension. A koan, assigned or naturally arisen, takes over and the person is grasped by intense searching. Finally there is a strong—even tremendous—breakthrough, followed by an often extended period of integration of the light into the person's psychology and behavioral patterns.

On the gradual path to enlightenment, the steps are not as large and intense, and there aren't as many fireworks, just a steady growth in small increments of insight and integration. I often speak of the gradual path as that of the commonplace kensho. There are little insights, shifts of consciousness that take place in our lives all the time. Sometimes we hardly perceive them, but they are real growth. I also feel that a very great deal of progress goes on within us at a level we are not aware of at all. I often ask audiences to not sell themselves short and remind them that they are all enlightened to some degree, that the phenomenon of commonplace kensho is actually quite common. The important thing is to remain faithful to one's practice. Much as I would like to have some fireworks, my way does seem to be the gradual path.

In spiritual direction, I am often surprised by what comes out of my mouth at times. Even more amazing is how I seem to know where people are when they talk about their really deep experiences. I seem to *recognize* what has happened, as if somehow I've been there myself. I won't try to unpack this phenomenon, but I do seem to have light within me. Those six years of formal zen training actually did change my consciousness profoundly. Yamada Roshi saw this. I've continued on with zazen on my own (but with hundreds of truly wonderful companion meditators), and my awareness continues to gradually change in many enriching ways. For one thing, (and I mean it seriously), I no longer kill mosquitoes!

PART TWO

COMING BACK

Two roads diverged in a wood and I
I took the one less traveled by
And that has made all the difference.
Robert Frost

Chapter 11

A MASSIVE CHANGE

Nothing is so sacred
That it cannot, need not change
And remain the same

T he main reason that I returned to the United States in 1982 was because I felt like a fake. It was true that in all my ministry in Japan, I was saying and teaching fine things about the spiritual path, but at the same time, I was racked by the self-accusation that I was not speaking from experience. There were even times after giving a conference on prayer or the scriptures that I was practically sick to my stomach, because I felt so strongly that my actual experience did not match my intellect and its words. I often thought of the scribes and Pharisees of the gospels. They are presented as teaching not from experience but from the words of the Bible and their own intellectual interpretations. Jesus, on the other hand, taught "as one who had authority, and not as the scribes" (Mk. 1:22), the authority of personal experience.

Regardless of how valid this problem was objectively, it was very real for me. It spread out into most of the facets of my life and built up such tension in me that something had to give. Finally, I asked for and was granted a kind of informal leave of absence from teaching at Sophia Junior College, from all other ministries, and even from living in a Jesuit community. I returned to the States and, as it were, bummed around for many months. As seriously as I could, I meditated, read, and prayed.

Gradually, circumstances led me to direct a meditation day here, a semi-retreat there. Since, after a full year, I was still feeling rather shaky about my whole way of life, a good Jesuit classmate, Gene Zimmers, invited me to attend the renewal program at the School of Applied Theology of the Graduate Theological Union in Berkeley. This course was truly helpful, and at its conclusion in late spring of 1984, it became clear that I was not to return to Japan. It was then that I moved across San Francisco Bay to join the staff of Mercy Center in Burlingame. Fifty years before, during the Great Depression, these very Sisters had taken me into their school for almost nothing. It was high time to directly pay back a little of the debt I owed them.

The two years plus since landing at the San Francisco airport had been a difficult time for me. But I had hung on through the rebellion, confusion, and pain, while the Spirit worked through movements both inside and outside me. In general, I followed my gut rather than my head, and ended up starting the next great phase of my life. This marginal man with one foot on either side of the Pacific was now to become a bridge on the spiritual path joining East and West, to, I hope, the benefit of both.

As I gradually adapted to life in the U.S., one thing became clear, There is a deeply felt dissatisfaction in the hearts of many Christians. For example, the movements begun by the Vatican Council II for greater place for the laity at every level of the Catholic Church life seemed to me to be engendering in thousands of people a longing for deeper spirituality and, for those who had gone to Eastern religions to fulfill this longing, a need to integrate all that they had experienced together with their Christian roots. Ever since coming to Mercy Center, I have been working with such people in a highly ecumenical and inter-religious effort toward the revitalization of both our humanity and Christianity. There are many movements in Christian churches today that are working toward renewal. I am convinced that one of the most important is that which learns from the profound enlightenment of Eastern spiritual heritages. *Like all elements in creation, Christianity must evolve.*

It was early January, 1984. A small group of us from the Graduate Theological Union were attending a large Buddhist-Christian dialogue conference in Hawaii. When we arrived at the conference, I found that quite a number of Japanese and Chinese participants were attending, and I enjoyed the renewed contact with Eastern thought and culture. Hawaii itself had so much of the Orient woven into the fabric of its lifestyle. On a crowded bus once, I was delighted to see second- or third-generation Japanese schoolgirls get up and give their seats to elderly people. This is something I had seen, even benefited from, so often in Japan. I still have many memories of the talks and individual meetings at the conference, but what has stayed with me the most is the conference theme. It was all about paradigm shift, the need for a new paradigm on which to build a whole new world. The movement toward such a shift continues to swell around the world.

In his insightful book *Person in Cosmos*, the Australian Catholic priest Kevin O'Shea writes:

> This would, in all, suggest that *a* new sense of Godness is arising in our cultural consciousness. Assertions about the femininity of God, and of change in God, are only steps along the way to a massive paradigm change about God, in which we are using our brains differently. We are on the threshold of a new understanding of contemplation itself. Its price is a changing notion of person, and a changing notion of cosmos.[1]

Notice the areas that O'Shea focuses on as he describes the massive paradigm shift: Godness or God, person, cosmos, and contemplation. These are exactly the areas I will be taking up in this Part Two of this book. To O'Shea's list, I might only add, "a new Christ."

Before looking at these topics in detail, I feel that we need to focus more in general on the paradigm shift itself. How big a shift is needed? Where is it to come from? How can it happen? Is it even allowed in Christianity? Is it essential to the revitalization of Christianity?

How Big a Shift?

O'Shea speaks of "a massive paradigm change," especially about God. I couldn't agree more. There is no question that what is called for is a profound shift away from the model of human life that is built on the egocentric consciousness of our day to a wholeness-centered life. This may sound a bit vague, but it should become clearer as we go along.

There is much we can learn from the great Copernican paradigm change of over 400 years ago. For centuries and centuries, the earth was taken to be the center of the universe. Sun, moon, planets, and stars were seen to move around it in perfectly circular, regular orbits. The earth was fixed in its position and everything was seen as related to it. That was geocentrism.

From very early times in the West, there were people who saw the error of this prevailing cosmological paradigm. Nevertheless, even in scientific circles, the old, obvious construct held sway right up to the time of the European Renaissance. The Polish scholar Mikolay Kopernik (1473–1543) saw the problems of geocentrism, felt dissatisfied, and went to the early sources of astronomical knowledge. Above all, Copernicus (his Latin name) *carefully observed the cosmos itself.*

In the year of his death, his major work *De Revolutionibus Orbium Caelestium* (On the Revolving Movements of the Celestial Orbs) was published. In Copernicus's theory, the sun is in the center of the universe and the earth and the planets move around it in fixed, circular orbits. But even this great heliocentric paradigm shift was not complete. Kepler, Galileo, and Newton all added new elements and made revisions. This process is still going on. We now know that the whole solar system is only part of a much greater movement. Paradigm evolution never really ends.

The Center Must Shift

The first thing that we can learn from the Copernican revolution is that for a profound paradigm change, the integrating center of the construct must change. When the perceived center of the cosmos shifted from the earth to the sun, a whole new and more real experience of our world entered human consciousness. In our experience of self, for well over 4,000 years the human ego has been more or less the center of our vision of reality for most of humanity. All during this time, the voices of Buddha, Lao Tzu, Moses, the great Hindu mystics, Christ Jesus, Mohammed, and other such enlightened beings have proclaimed the error of egocentrism, but its widespread tyranny has continued right up to the present. Jesus' message was to deny your ego self and follow ME (True Self) into the reign of God. But how few have *really* done this.

The Shift Takes Time

In astronomy, the old geocentrism dominates our ordinary consciousness even today. Though we all learn the Copernican truth in grade school, we don't say that the earth turns each morning to face the sun; we still say that the sun rises to face us on earth. This is pure geocentrism. The fundamental teaching about the human self was presented by Jesus two millennia ago, yet egocentrism remains rampant. How long will the shift take from the little local self to the God-centered paradigm for human living?

I believe that we have the opportunity for a huge reduction of this lag as we move into the twenty-first century. The astounding acceleration of change even in the twentieth century is apparent to everyone. However, because of the Internet and other amazing means of communication, the rate of change increases by quantum leaps each year. The actual possibility of a massive paradigm shift for all humanity is right here before us. This is all tremendously exciting. What must we do to insure its appropriate realization?

What Copernicus Did, So Must We

Copernicus came to his great paradigm change *in himself first*. Three basic elements allowed this to happen for him.

First, he wasn't afraid to admit the problems inherent in geocentrism. He allowed himself to feel disturbing dissatisfaction. He did this in spite of certain opposition from some people in the scientific community and ecclesiastical authorities. Geocentrism is clearly expressed in the Bible, so the churches were bound to object to his theories. Copernicus was a Catholic, but he allowed himself to feel profound levels of both dissatisfaction and nagging need for change. He went deeply into the problem, even though it meant revamping or rejecting much of what he had learned up to then. More and more people today are also acknowledging paradigm problems, deep dissatisfactions about Christianity, and immense need for evolutionary change—first in themselves, and then in the Western mind-set.

Second, Copernicus turned to the contemplation of the heavens themselves. He tuned into their reality with an open heart and mind. So also must we do today. Leaving ourselves open, we must face up to the reality of our ultimate Self, even though this may mean that we will lose ourselves in the seemingly dark emptiness of the Source. Enlightenment and salvation can only come from plunging into the darkness under the bodhi tree or the olive trees of Gethsemane.

Finally, Copernicus employed the highest levels of scientific consciousness available to him. He used the best instruments of his day, and studied the scientific literature in which this advanced knowledge was presented. He came to his shift through the influence of advanced knowledge in mathematics and astronomical investigation. For the needed paradigm shift in our view of self, Source, and the Cosmos to actually happen, we must submit ourselves to the powerful influence of the highest levels of advanced consciousness. The subtle, the causal, and the non-dual stages of awareness are eminently available to us today. They are expressed in many sacred scriptures and sacramental liturgies. The disciplines of mindfulness and meditation are being taught and practiced everywhere. The stage is set for our personal paradigm change, and for that of the whole human race.

The Need for Mysticism

The new paradigm about the cosmos, self, and God can only arise from a mode of perception which advances beyond our ordinary, scientific, discriminatory thinking, and works out the new mind-set from there. This new level of "contemplation" that O'Shea speaks of is called mysticism. We must open ourselves out to the influence of the highest level of mystical perception available to us. Our revitalization and growth must arise out of non-dual awareness. To actually create the new paradigm, the non-dual person will use the verbal expression skills and the scientific, philosophical, and theological advances made on the lower stages of consciousness evolution. Nevertheless, it only makes sense to follow the highest level of perception, and that is non-dual mysticism.

Opposition

The Copernican revolution was opposed by many people of good will. So, too, there is bound to be powerful opposition to the great paradigm shift of the post-modern era. Probably this opposition will come from many groups with obvious good will such as conservative churches and scripture-based fundamentalist groups, perhaps from the scientific community, and from all those elements in the general culture which cherish stability and are uncomfortable with radical change. Such groups perform the necessary and important functions of putting the brakes on overly rapid change and forestalling future shock.

In general, the greatest opposition will arise from the pervading ego-based consciousness still prevalent and certainly present to some degree in all of us. The law of change is that death to one stage is an absolute prerequisite for movement to a new stage. But the ego certainly doesn't want to relinquish its central dominance. It does not want to die. Yet nothing other than this great death can create the shift. The lines are drawn. The evolutionary challenge is ringing out, out of the depths of our own being.

An Evolving Christianity

Must Christianity change? Can it change and still remain what it is? These are very big questions, about which whole books could be written. Here it will suffice to offer a few basic ideas, which will be applied and exemplified in subsequent chapters.

The inexorable but glorious law of constant change is apparent everywhere in the universe. As the ancient Greek philosopher Heraclitus said, *"Panta rei, ouden de menei."* Everything flows and nothing abides. The question, then, is not whether Christianity must change. Of course it must. In the sixties, Pope John XXIII recognized this and called for *"aggiornamento"* (updating). Rather, the question is what can change? And what must remain so that Christianity itself remains?

Religion is difficult to define, but most experts seem to agree that a religion is constituted by the four "C's": creed, code, cult, and community. This clear, simple description of the components of a religion is helpful but, I would say, gravely inadequate. All four of these elements are derivative. They arise from a prior and essential foundation, the religious experience of the founder or founders. If this quintessential, live experience ever disappears from a religious tradition, it will dry up and hopefully fade away.

A true experience of the divine—the kind on which a religious movement can be based—is always beyond words. It follows that the instinctively chosen language used to express the experience will be open-ended, containing right-brain expressions such as symbols, stories, poetry, paradoxes, and parables. Because these are non-defining, all-inclusive, and expansive in nature, they can lead one to the ineffable experience itself, especially when they are used by an enlightened person to communicate experience.

When, through such vital communication, a number of people come to basically share the same experience, they naturally come together to form a *community*. It follows that they will create a simple liturgy, a *cult*, for their gatherings. It is this basic form of a religion that is well expressed in the popular description of the Catholic mass, "Gather the people. Tell the story. Break the bread."

It is obvious, then, how two of the four "C's" derive from a common religious experience. The third, *code*, is created because, as the number of community gatherings grows, some practical and common regulations about the liturgy become necessary; thus, the formation of the liturgical law. At the same time, prescriptions about the lifestyle that is necessary for the promotion and preservation of the experience are expressed in a moral and ethical code.

A highly developed *creed* is the last of the four to arise. It is a product of our differentiating, categorizing mind. This mind is not satisfied with poetry, stories, and symbols. It possesses a powerful drive to put the ineffable into manageable mental boxes. This is a very human drive, and creeds are helpful and important. But at the same time, creedal formulas can be dangerous, because it is so easy for us to substitute an intellectual grasp of the creed for existential participation in the foundational experience. Mental understanding can even hinder our evolutionary advance to higher-level consciousness of the divine.

Upon reflection, it is clear that all four of the "C's" can and must change with the flow of history. What cannot change in Christianity is the following of Christ Jesus into divine experience. Christian faith is the entrustment of one's whole being—body, mind, will, and soul—to Christ, who is "the pioneer and perfecter of our faith." (Heb. 12:2) Everything else in Christianity can and must evolve with the times. Creedal formulas, to the degree that they present this basic essence of Christianity, are not open to change. But inasmuch as they are the intellectual formulation of this essence, they always need periodic updating. In his classic book *Creeds in the Making*, Alan Richardson states:

> In the second place, the realization that the essence of the Christian religion is belief in a person rather than in a doctrine or system of ideas explains why doctrines must be reformulated for every generation, and why no particular system of doctrine can be ever final. Every age must make afresh its own interpretation of the central fact of history.

That fact remains the same, but our view of its significance changes, develops, deepens and expands.[2]

And Karl Rahner, in a wonderful address on the occasion of his seventy-fifth birthday said:

> From this more critical distance, I envisage a theology which in the Church at large must be the theology of a worldwide Church. That means a theology which does not only recite its own medieval history, but one that can listen to the wisdom of the East, to the longing for freedom in Latin America, and also to the sound of African drums.[3]

The Zen Witness

Zen is alleged to be atheistic, or at least non-theistic, but I have found that zen has immense things to say about God. Before presenting my theological suggestions, I would like to offer what I learned about God from zen. To act as a zen spokesperson, I would like to introduce an imaginary character named Doshin. In the dialog of the next two chapters you can, if you wish, take the part of the questioner, who is Christian. The chapters are called "Doshin Iwaku." *Iwaku* is an old-style zen word that means to say, to speak. It is often used in koans. So let's hear what Doshin has to say.

Chapter 12

DOSHIN SAYS: I

From a rice land
The seed boldly grows to
A wheat harvest

You, the questioner, are on an airplane flight from the U.S. Midwest to San Francisco. Beside you is an Asian man dressed in what you suspect are the robes of a Buddhist monk. You know he speaks English from the way he spoke to the flight attendant. You are curious, so...

Questioner: I can see by your robes that you must be a monk. Is that right? Are you a Buddhist?

Monk: Yes. I'm a Japanese zen monk.

Q: Are you with a zen group in the San Francisco Bay Area? I know several of them.

M: No, I am with a zendo in the Midwest. Ten years ago, I was sent by my temple in Japan to help a group of Americans who had asked for a zen teacher. Right now, I'm on my way to see a publisher in San Francisco, and then I'll continue on for a visit to Japan.

Q: Oh. You've written a book? What is it about?

M: Actually, I wrote it first in Japanese, but people at the zendo wanted to translate it into English, so we got together and this is what resulted. (The monk takes out a manuscript from a briefcase under the seat in front of him and hands it to you.) The Japanese title is *Komugi No Kariire*, which is literally translated as "A Wheat Harvest." The zen group likes the title because we are in the wheat belt.

Q: That's fascinating. Why do you say "Harvest"?

M: Because it's about what I received and learned here in the heartland of the United States. It has been a wonderful time for me. I wrote the book to tell all my Japanese confrères and friends what I've learned.

Q: I see that your name is Doshin. What does it mean?

M: That's my Zen name. It's composed of two ideograms. *Do* means way or path. It refers to the Path of Buddha. *Shin* means heart or core. You are free to put those two together any way you wish: the heart of the Path, Path with a heart, whatever.

Q: That's beautiful.

M: Actually, there are two other ways the sound "Do" could be written. Sometimes I write or think of my name using one of these other ideograms. One of them means "the same." Written this way, Doshin means "of the same heart and mind as you." If I write Do another way, it means "a child's heart" or "naïveté."

Q: That's fascinating. Do zen monks often play with their names that way?

M: No, not very often, I'd say. But I have a rather adventuresome spirit. Probably that is why I was sent to America. Even while I've been here, I did something zen monks hardly, if ever, do. I went to a Jesuit university and studied philosophy and theology.

Q: My gosh. That really does sound unusual. Do you write about that adventure in your book?

M: Oh yes. That is what the book is mainly about. That and my life with Western practitioners. Wheat is not native to Japan, so, although we grow it, it is still felt to be something Western. I took what I've harvested during my time in this wheat culture and especially what I learned at the University, put it together with my zen and Japanese mentality and wrote the book. Above all, I talk about God.

Q: Oh! Tell me more.

M: My father was a zen priest in charge of a temple in Okayama Prefecture, west of Osaka. So I grew up in a Buddhist atmosphere. I never understood what Christians said about God, but I was interested. My questions about the Christian God only got bigger and deeper during the time I was studying scholastic philosophy with the Jesuits. All I could find were a lot of seeming contradictions.

For some reason, probably it was just my perverse nature, I didn't want to get into modern philosophy. I chose classes in the more ancient scholastic philosophy. The classes weren't large. One Jesuit teacher, Father Huber, was especially kind. He helped me a lot, even got me a scholarship. I think he found it interesting to have a Zen monk as a student. Anyway, even in those classes, I found that God was described as an absolute being, as pure, complete existence, as infinite.

Q: Yes. That's what we always say. What's wrong with those ideas?

M: Actually, it took some time for my real questions and problems to arise. They didn't fully surface until I began theology. During philosophy classes, I was still Doshin in the sense of being settled at the heart of the Buddhist path. When I began theology, I decided to be the open, naïve Doshin. Almost at once, one big problem became clear.

Q: What was that? I'm a Christian, but I admit I don't understand God very well.

M: As I said, both philosophy and theology describe God as the perfect, infinite Being. On the other hand, all creatures great and small are said to be very finite, limited beings. Usually, very imperfect. Now, the whole goal of human life is described as union with God. My simple question is how can a finite being become one with Infinite Being? If the human becomes infinite, then it is no longer finite. It is infinite like God. That is not union of two beings. The human side is eliminated. Or, if the Infinite actually becomes a finite human being, then the Infinite is eliminated.

I know that you call the incarnation of the Divine Being as a human being a mystery. I don't want to be impolite, but to me, it is not a mystery (a truth, as you say, which we cannot fully understand), but rather a mystification of the impossible. On the one hand, we have an actual way of being that is unlimited, unbounded in any way. On the other, there is a mode of being that is essentially limited. These two modes of being are incompatible. Again, I ask you, how can Infinite *Being* and finite *being* become one without the destruction of one side? Union is two becoming one, while remaining two.

Along this same line is the problem I have of God being totally other to us. Because God is said to be infinite and we finite, God is spoken of as *the other*. Given the absolute other-ness between divine nature and human nature, how can we become one with God?

Q: Well. I have to admit that these do seem like problems. I've never thought it all out like you. What does Zen say? Do you speak about infinite and finite beings?

M: We speak of form and emptiness. In my mind, these two are equivalent to finite and infinite. But *we don't speak of them as "beings."* That is the crucial point. Form (finite) and emptiness (infinite) are not distinct beings. They are distinct constituents of being. To describe enlightenment in philosophical terms, these are what is seen. Full enlightenment always includes an experience of both emptiness and form. This emptiness is not nothing. It is no-thing-ness.

Q: Not nothing but no-thing-ness! Aren't they the same? I, too, don't want to be impolite, but isn't that mystification?

M: I admit it does sound like I'm indulging in contradiction, but what I'm trying to say by "no-thing-ness" is that the Void that Zen discovers is not a being. It is an inexpressible, formless, *constituent* of being. It is pure *potency*, whereas form is *act*. I came to really like those philosophical terms. I think that they shed light on what Zen enlightenment is. The Void is infinite power to manifest itself in an unlimited number of limited ways. Any and all possible forms are contained in the Emptiness potentially.

Q: So you are saying that what you discover in satori is the infinite, but it's not infinite being?

M: That's right. It's not a being. Satori or enlightenment shows us the infinite source of being. Just one of the three constituents of being.

Q: Three constituents?

M: Yes, three. But I've gotten ahead of myself. Let's go back to kensho, the first experience of enlightenment. The Void is experienced as the Source of all form beings. Pure potency manifests itself in the myriad of finite beings, the form world, the world of phenomena. A form is an act of the pure potency. Form is act. Emptiness is potency. I've been surprised at how helpful these philosophical terms are when speaking to my Zen group and to other Westerners. Are you following me?

Q: I think I am. I sat with a zen group once. I know about kensho and I remember the emptiness and form referred to in the Heart Sutra. You are saying that form is also a constituent of being.

M: Exactly. Every existent being is Formless/Form. Since you've been to a zendo, you'll know that we are always chanting the Heart Sutra. It is a short sutra that contains the heart of *prajna*. Prajna is the intuitive wisdom that arises from true enlightenment. The whole sutra is built around the discovery of pure emptiness or *shunyata* and around the insight: "Form, that is emptiness. Emptiness, that is form." Form and Emptiness are *one* because they are two constituents making up being. As human beings, you and I are Formless/Form beings.

Q: But you spoke of three constituents. And where is God in all this? Does Buddhism deny God?

M: Let's take the matter of the third constituent first. Actually, it is indicated in your English word *being*. This "ing" expresses action or movement. Being is dynamic. It is moving. There is only being when the Formless Source *moves* into form, into act. Without this movement, there is no being. So movement is the third constituent or component of being. I like to call this movement The Flow. The Flow is circular. Source to form, and then form back to Source. Only by returning to the Source can a being rise to a higher state, receive more life. This is at the heart of evolution.

Q: All this is very intriguing. Is this the way zen has always explained reality?

M: Oh, no. These are Western terms, but to me, they are most helpful in describing the intuition of being or enlightenment. This is what I have written in *Komugi No Kariire* for my friends in Japan. If you are a Christian, you will be interested to know that none of this became clear to me until I encountered the doctrine of the Trinity in theology.

Q: The Trinity! Amazing. To me, the Trinity is not clear at all. So that's where God comes into all this?

M: Yes, exactly. But what I have come up with is not the usual Christian description of the Trinity. In fact, I am developing a new paradigm for describing all reality and it is based on the Trinity. When we took the theology of the Trinity with Father Huber, I was the simple, open-minded, naïve Doshin. As I learned more about this teaching, I even turned into the third Doshin, the one who is of the same mind and heart as you.

Q: So you actually accept the teaching of the Trinity? You really are an adventuresome zen monk.

M: No, I couldn't accept it exactly as it was taught. Again, God was said to be Infinite *Being*. Also, there was no potency in God. They said that God is only pure act. That the very essence of God is pure existence. Well, for the life of me, I couldn't see how there could be relations in such a God. And the Three Persons *are* in relationship. For a relationship, there have to be two or more who share in something together. You and I are in a companion relationship because we share this flight to San Francisco. But you and I are distinct human beings. No distinction, no relationship. But the Father, Son, and Holy Spirit are not distinct beings. God is one being. Then what are the Three? To me, the only possible answer is that they are constituents of being. The constituent called the Father (the Formless), and the constituent called the Son (the universal Form) share one being, the Spirit (the Movement). Thus, the Trinity!

Father Huber explained that hypostasis is the word that the Greek Fathers of your Church used for person in the Trinity. *Hypo* means under and *stasis* means standing. So a hypostasis is what stands under being. I like that. Etymologically, at least, hypostasis sounded to me like the constituents of being, Formless Source and Form in Movement, Potency in Action.

Q: But to describe God as Potency Moving into Act doesn't sound like the Christian Teaching at all to me.

M: Yes, I can understand your feelings. You were probably brought up on the Nicene Creed. I had never even heard of this creed until I went to theology class. When I first read it, it made no sense to me at all. I couldn't grasp those thought patterns, because they were so different from mine. Then I was told that the creeds from Nicea and Chalcedon were conceptual formulations carefully worked out by faith joined to Greek and Roman modes of thought. As soon as Fr. Huber said they were conceptual, I was relieved.

In zen, concepts are not considered the highest form of knowledge. They are indirect knowing and are quite unreliable. They are only attempts to express what has been experienced directly. Even great philosophical systems are ultimately only attempts and must be used lightly and with detachment. Real experience is better expressed in simple, concrete words or images and in poetry.

Q: Well, that's what our gospels do, wouldn't you say?

M: Precisely. So that's where I turned. I read all four of the gospels slowly and carefully. I got really excited. "It's all here!" I kept saying to myself, "It's all here! Jesus truly was supremely enlightened."

Oh, oh. The attendants are distributing lunch. I'll have to be brief. I'll just say a word or two about some trinitarian texts I discovered in the gospels. First, "...so that you may not appear to be fasting except to your Father who is hidden." (Mt. 6:6) The Father is the Formless Source and is hidden in formlessness.

Secondly, "No one comes to the Father except through me...Whoever has seen me has seen the Father." (Jn. 14:6 & 9) The Father/Source is invisible. The Son/Form is visible. The Source is only known in form-manifestation. They are different and distinct constituents, but one being. "The Father and I are one." (Jn. 10:30)

Finally, "Go therefore and make disciples of all nations, baptizing them in the name of the Father and of the Son and of the Holy Spirit." (Mt.

28:19) Fr. Huber explained that *shem*, the Hebrew word for "name," is very dynamic. It's rooted in the word for a movement, a flow, or a stream. So for a Christian to be baptized is to be plunged into the Flow of the Source and the Form in Movement. The movement is the Holy Spirit. The Spirit is said to proceed from the Father and the Son. I take this to mean that there is Movement from the Source into Form; then Movement from the Form back to the Source. That is the nature of all reality. *There is only the Flow.*

Christians seem to believe that at their baptism they receive eternal life for the first time and become children of God. I have problems with that way of thinking. When zen teachers talk to Christians, they sometimes describe kensho as a baptism, because in enlightenment, a person's consciousness is plunged into awareness of the True Self that has always been within. It is just as it was at the baptism of Jesus. For him, it was a knowledge event. He was told, "You are my Beloved Son." He was not newly made into the Son of the Father. His True Self was revealed to his awareness. So it is with any Christian baptism, I'd say. It is a revelation of what you already are. The newness is in the awareness and in the integrating of one's whole life according to this Self-realization.

So the Trinity of Infinite Potency in Movement into Act, these three components of reality form the paradigm I would like to offer to Christians and Buddhists alike, not just to describe God but all reality.

Before the lady comes with our lunch, I want to give you a printout of a chapter from the *Tao Te Ching* of the great Taoist mystic Lao Tzu. About 2,400 years ago, he said all this much better than I can. We still use his insights in zen. I gave this page to my zen students. I've added some numbers to connect it to some ideas of the paradigm that I'm offering.

Entering into utmost emptiness
I maintain the stillness wholeheartedly. [1]
All things are moving together,
Thus I contemplate their cyclic movement. [2]

So many, many things!
Each returns to the source.
Returning to the source is called silence.
Silence is called the return to life. [3]
Returning to life is called the eternal state.
To know the eternal is called enlightenment.

When one does not know the eternal, blindness causes disaster. [4]
Knowing the eternal, one becomes one with all. [5]
Being one with all, one is without attachment.
Being without attachment, one becomes ruler. [6]
Becoming ruler, one becomes divine. [7]
Becoming divine, one becomes the flow of life.
Becoming the flow of life, one becomes imperishable. [8]
And even the dissolution of the body is not destruction.

Tao Te Ching, Chapter 16 (Author's Translation)

Notes:
1. Ox picture #8
2. Ox picture #9. Formless to Form. Father to Son
3. Ox picture #9
4. Ego-centric consciousness
5. Satori
6. The kikunushi
7. The One Responsible Doer
8. Spirit – Life. Resurrection.

Chapter 13

DOSHIN SAYS: II

At the heart of thee
We find not an Other
But simply me

L unch is over. You've thought about Doshin's ideas and have read the passage from Lao Tzu.)

Q: What you said is extremely interesting, Doshin. See if I have your new paradigm correctly. All reality is only the one Flow. This is the Flow of the Formless into Form and Form back to the Source. The Source is infinite potency. Every form manifestation is an existential act of this potency. One Source, many manifestations. The Flow is the Holy Spirit. These three are not distinct beings; they are constituents of all being. In fact, to put it in my terms, the Source-and-the-Form-in-Movement constitute the bipolar energy field of all reality.

However, I have some questions. Let's say two main problems. First of all, if you say that there is nothing but the Flow, isn't that pantheism? I have heard it said that Buddhism is atheistic, that, in effect, it pretty much denies the reality of God. Now you seem to be saying that there is *only* God!

M: I think I understand your problem. A number of people have challenged me in the same way. To begin with, please remember what I am doing. I am trying to use both Western concepts like potency and act and also Christian scripture-based teachings such as the Trinity to restate Buddhist insights. I have been doing this for our American zen group. Also, I wrote this book for zen people in Japan. Zen has rarely, if ever, spoken about itself in these terms. On the other hand, what I've worked out does seem to restate Christianity as well.

Pantheism says that everything is God. It identifies God and the universe. First, we must certainly admit that in a system of thought that places God as the Infinite Other to all creatures and creatures as finite others to God, pantheism is a total contradiction. It's unthinkable. But I would maintain that in such a system, union with God is also a contradiction. Again, it all comes down to *what you mean by God.*

Secondly, I think your problem about pantheism would no longer be a problem if Christians took more seriously, perhaps, what is written in your great scriptures. I am especially thinking of what is said about two things: eternal life and sharing the divine nature.

Q: Oh? Do you think that our teaching about everlasting life is somewhat pantheistic?

M: Notice what you just did. You substituted everlasting for eternal. To me, that is confusing. Everlasting could mean that a life starts and then continues forever. But that is not eternal life. Eternal has neither end *nor beginning.* This point is crucial. I'm sure we can agree that eternal life is God's life, divine life. Union with God and possessing eternal life mean the same thing. If you follow the ordinary Christian thought system, both *entry into* union with God and *entering* eternal life seem to me to be contradictory. As I understand Christian thought, there is the same difference between eternal and temporal life as there is between God and creatures. It is a difference *in be-ing.*

Therefore, if you enter eternal life, your temporal life has to cease. What's more, if you enter eternal life, *your* participation in eternal life has a beginning. Zen says that you already are eternal life. "Entry" into divine life is an awareness event. You become conscious of what your life already is. All life is eternal/temporal. Incidentally, I remember that Fr. Huber once quoted St. Augustine in Latin: "Quod aeternum non est, nihil est." (What is not eternal, is nothing.) I'm sorry I didn't have time to ask him more about that quotation.

Q: We say that in baptism, we *become* children of God, whereas we were not before baptism. And we say that then we possess the grace that can *lead* us *to* eternal life in heaven. You seem to be saying that even without baptism, everyone is already born of God with God's eternal life.

M: Exactly. That is just what I am saying. Eternal does not mean a long, long time. Eternal means outside time altogether. So it doesn't compete with time! Just as each of us is Formless/Form Flow, so we are each Eternal/Temporal Flow. There is no incompatibility between time and eternity, form and formless, because they are not beings. They are components of being. Our actual life is always and ultimately eternal/temporal. We are very conscious of being in time. To become aware of ourselves as eternal is "entry" into eternal life.

Q: Then the deification of humanity that the Eastern Christians speak of is simply a matter of becoming aware of what we already are and then living a divine life.

M: That's right. What you just said about deification brings up the matter of sharing in God's nature. Fr. Huber took this up one day and gave us many quotations. I've used two of them in *A Wheat Harvest*. One is from the Second Letter of Peter. It says that God has given us promises, so that through them we "may come to share in the divine nature." (2 Peter 1:4) The other quote is from the Catholic Mass. When the priest pours a little water into the cup of wine, he says, "By the mystery of this water and wine, may we come to share in the divinity of Christ, who humbled himself to share in our humanity."

You may be used to hearing such statements, but when I heard them for the first time, they were immensely impressive. They say that we are literally divine. I can't help but think of the zen expression kensho jobutsu. Kensho means to experientially see (ken) the true nature (sho) of yourself and all things. When you do this, you become (jo) a buddha (butsu), in the sense that to yourself, you seem to become what you now realize you always were.

Q: So in your paradigm of reality, we are born sharing in God's nature just as we all live eternal life from birth. It's just that we don't know what we are.

M: Thank you. You can put these things better than I can. You know, I was reading St. Paul's letter to the Ephesians one day and came across a sentence where he says, "He destined us for adoption as his children through Jesus Christ." (Eph. 1:5) I can't help but feel that that is a very unfortunate expression. An *adopted* child of God could never be said to share in divine *nature.* There seem to be two strains in Christian texts. Some accent our distance from God. Others teach God/human oneness. Your Christian mystic, Julian of Norwich, says: "To seek God without already having him is of all things the most impossible." But you said you had two problems. Perhaps, we've said enough about the problem of pantheism. What was your other problem?

Q: It has to do with God as personal. My cousin speaks about God as "the Big Boss upstairs." It's just his way of referring to God and I rather resonate with it, because it is personal. To talk about God as Formless Source Moving into Form-manifestation seems terribly impersonal to me.

M: Yes, one of our zen practitioners had the same objection. First of all, let me say that I certainly hold that God is personal. The Divine Source is intelligent and knows how to *act* according to the divine nature. An intelligent, responsible doer is a person. God is a vast, unlimited Person, because the Person's power of action is unlimited. This is the "one True Person of no rank" that the great zen master Rinzai speaks of. It is awfully hard to speak about this divine Person in English because we have to use either She, He or It. All these put God into a limited category and are false designations.

Take the very enlightening text where Moses meets God on Mount Sinai the time he was attracted by the burning bush. (Exodus 3) God made a

Self revelation to Moses! When Moses asked what he should respond when the Israelites asked for the name of the God who sent him, God replied, "Thus shall you say to the Israelites, I AM has sent me to you." This was Moses' great enlightenment experience. He came to know the "Person of no rank."

The people of that time had many gods. It was still the age of the gods. There was the god of fertility who produced the harvest and gave children, the god who waged war, the god who gave peace, the god of the sea, the god of this nation or that. But this was a revelation of the God of Being. This is the God who is simply the great I AM. Wherever there is "is-ing," this God is responsible. This is the one Doer in all creation. The Person who is doing everything. So God is essentially personal. That is no problem.

Please don't think of the Source as a big impersonal power running everything. The Source I speak of is an intelligent, loving, personal power. The very essence of the Source is to give life, to manifest. In philosophy, one of the professors liked to quote the Latin phrase *bonum est diffusivum sui.* Good is diffusive of itself. The Source wants only to flow out into form manifestation. This is love, total self-giving. Though we are many, we are all One Flow. We live in love. Rejoice in Yahweh, the One-Who-Is.

Q: Oh. There's San Francisco Bay. We'll land in a few minutes. Thank you so much, Doshin. You've made this into a wonderful flight. I'm sure your book will help many people. I'll tell all my friends about it. You have certainly inspired me. Now, I want to study my Christianity again.

M: Thank you for listening so beautifully. I realize that my new paradigm may disturb some people, but I offer it in gratitude. Besides coming to appreciate Christianity more deeply, I've also gotten a new understanding of zen.

But please treat all this lightly. The important thing is experience, not intellectual reflection. There is a simple Japanese saying, *Sumeba, miyako.* (When you live, capital.) When you live somewhere, it becomes your capital. Really be attentive and live to the fullest right where you are, and that place will become your Camelot, your place of divine life and joy. What is urgent is to live, not to think.

Chapter 14

God Talk I

Standing in the East
Looking West, saying
"God is different."

I t was one September morning in 1969. I had been working on something at my desk in my room at our language school in Kamakura. After two hours I needed a break, so I went up to walk on the roof of our residence. It was almost six months since I had begun formal training in zen, and no doubt it had already begun its powerful impact on my consciousness. I wasn't thinking of anything in particular as I walked down to the West end of the roof and just gazed at a not-so-beautiful bank of clouds in the sky.

Suddenly I realized that *God is different*. There was a shift in my consciousness. Nothing spectacular, just a realization that God is different from all that I had conceived about "Him" up to that point. I wasn't excited, but as I walked back down to my room and as I went through the rest of that day, I kept repeating to myself, God is different! God is different!

Now, as I look back, I know that that moment of insight was one of the great events of my life. It was one of the richest fruits of my "going over," a major step on my pilgrimage. Since I have always been interested even intellectually in God, the changes of consciousness initiated by that shift have deeply affected my whole outlook on reality. In fact, the struggle to accept, elucidate, and develop that intuition has been a large part of my life story ever since that day. It was a crucial step toward the development of a whole new paradigm of reality.

God is Different

The fact that this change in my attitude toward God began along with my Zen initiation is, I feel, illuminating. Some people say that there is no God in Buddhism. I do not accept that idea at all. Once my mind was cleared of attachment to the purely Western notions of God, my experience of Buddhism was able to teach me God in a wonderful way. It brought me to experience God. So, again, I propose to employ the insights I've received in Zen to expound my experience and understanding of Divine Being. As a teacher of many years, I feel it might be helpful to sketch in outline all that I want to say about God before plunging in:

What God *is not*:
- God is not other to us as we are to each other.
- God is not one within a series. Not just the first in a hierarchy of beings.

What God *is*:
- God is truly a person, the Subject responsible for everything.
- The Ultimate is bipolar, the coincidence of opposites.
- God is Three-In-One (a Trinity).

God and Us:
- The Divine Being is holographically present in all beings.
- We are holons within the Divine Whole. We creatures all exist in God and God in us.

- As holons, our self-identification must include divinity. We, too, are bipolar beings, the coincidence of opposites.
- God is the Universal Energy Form Field.
- God is in process.

You have probably already noticed, and you will certainly see as you read along, that this God is "different" from the God you likely grew up with. The outline also presents a different vision of ourselves and reality. Now let's look at some of these ideas in more detail.

God Is Not Other To Us

How much my consciousness about God has changed over the years was powerfully brought home to me in Minnesota. In the fall and early winter of 1996, I spent four wonderful months with a small group of research scholars at the Institute for Ecumenical and Cultural Research, St. John's University in Collegeville, Minnesota. In several of our discussions, the concept of God as "The Great Other" came up.

One of the latest thinkers to stress this concept of God was the Swiss theologian Karl Barth, who insisted that God is *totaliter aliter*, totally other. Each time such an expression surfaced I was surprised at how strongly I reacted to it. All the other scholars seemed to peacefully accept this idea of the Divine. Possibly to them it seemed quite valid, traditional, and not to be challenged. For me, while I know that it has long been a part of Christian thinking about God, nevertheless it jarred acutely with all that I most identify with in both the Christian and Buddhist traditions. Actually, there are two points to be made here: (1) God is not totally other to us, and (2) God is not other to us as we are to each other.

Like nearly every western Christian, my education about Divinity was built on the assumption that we creatures are totally distinct from the Creator. God is infinite. We are finite. These two are contradictory and simply cannot be one. If you have boundaries, you cannot be boundless. We are totally distinct from and other to boundless Being. This is all perfectly logical. As long as you hold that there is a being that is exclusively infinite and other beings that are purely finite, then the two are completely different and opposite. However, as we shall see, there is no such reality as a purely infinite, formless *being*. Nor are we creatures purely finite, form beings! Much more of this as we go along.

Christians are always talking about our relationship to God. We are urged to relate to God as to our father, mother, friend, beloved, even judge. We all know that these words are basically all figures of speech when applied to the human-divine relationship. In their primary meanings, they refer to one human in relation to another human. But God is not just another human being. We say that we are in relation to "Him" (or "Her"), but this must be taken figuratively, not literally. One of the major purposes of this book is to try to get closer to literal reality.

Consider the confession of the modern Japanese zen master, Yamada Mumon. He writes that as a college student he felt a deep attraction to Christianity, but could not give himself to it because of the Christian anthropomorphic way of relating to God.

> While feeling an immense attraction to Christian teaching, the reason I did not follow it was "prayer." Prayer words simply do not come out from me. If I do use words, they seem to end up as false and nothing more than shallow sentimentality. If I invoke "My Father God," God becomes farther and farther away. The result is not the Absolute but a conceptual idol ....When I began to do zazen, I came to feel that it was zazen that was true prayer.
>
> (Author's translation)[1]

The first time I read these words close to thirty years ago, I didn't know what to do with them. I definitely resonated with Mumon Roshi's feelings, but wasn't ready to abandon saying the "Our Father." Also, as a priest, I am officially engaged in liturgical prayer *to* God. For years I went along in a semi-confused state. My experience of God and thoughts about God were evolving toward a mysterious oneness, but ordinary Christian prayer was holding me in "relationship" to the Other. I was well aware that all our images of God put "Him" into limiting categories. For me, they came to conceal more than reveal God. This personal ambiguity persisted well into the first years after I returned to the United States. However, before we can continue this subject on our relationship with the Divine, we must correct another common misapprehension about God.

Is God First?

We were always taught that we must love God first and above all. Creatures should always come second in our lives. In this model, there is a great hierarchical ranking in which God is first; then parents, spouses, and children; then friends and acquaintances; and on down the line through all animate creatures to rocks, stars, and the inanimate world. This God-first-and-above-all attitude was especially insisted on after I became a Jesuit. Vowed religious life in the Catholic church was explained as a style of life to which God chose a person as "His" special friend. Such a person should not give his or her heart to any creature, except as a way to love God, the Great Significant Other.

Notice, though, that in this scheme of things God is put into a kind of hierarchy with creatures. For true Christians, God always came first in this hierarchy. All others were arranged below in an ordered series. In this way of relating to God, we are using the same sense of distinction and even opposition that our relationship to creatures is based on. We are treating God as we treat our fellow creatures. God ends up being just a uniquely big and mysterious creature who is admittedly above all and loved first, but is still an anthropomorphized creature.

For some reason, the mistake in all this became clear to me during a T-group training session. It happened a year after the September morning on the roof described at the beginning of this chapter. I was attending a human relations workshop at Gotemba, a town near the foot of Mt. Fuji. Again, I experienced a quiet but deep shift in consciousness. I realized that contrary to our relationships with humans, God must not be put into a numbered series. God is not first among many, with the many arranged in ranks below. To do this is to reduce God to being just one of a gang, albeit *primus inter pares*—the first among equals. And once again, this conversion in my thinking probably happened because of zen, which, through the words of the great master Rinzai, was teaching me about the "true person of no rank."

At Gotemba, as I gazed up at Mt. Fuji from the lodge where we were staying, I knew that I had hit upon something important, but at the time was unable to do much with the insight. Now as I look back I can see it as another crucial step toward a whole new paradigm…not only about God but about all of reality.

Is God A Person?

An old caricature of Buddhism that was popular in the West until fairly recently was that of a monk sitting in contemplation of his navel and striving for nirvana, which was a kind of absorption of oneself in the *impersonal* Absolute. Naturally, when I entered the zendo I wondered about the seeming no-God character of Buddhism. As a cradle Christian, I felt something personal was lacking. As I recall, I handled this problem by simply not thinking about it. I concentrated on learning to meditate and listening to the unusual teaching. But the question remained: In zen, is the Ultimate a person? Does Buddhism in any sense have a personal God? Now, thirty years later, I can answer unhesitatingly "Yes, of course!" But the God of Buddhism (and of Christianity) is different from the personal friend to whom I relate in an ordinary human way. Return with me to the first formal Buddhist talk I ever heard.

It is *teisho* time at Jomyoji (the temple where I began zen). The bell has rung. The strident wooden clappers have sounded. An attendant has solemnly brought out the book containing the text for today's talk and placed it on a small stand in front of the sensei's cushion. After offering a stick of incense before the Buddhist image, Yamada Sensei takes his seat, quietly removes the formal silk covering from the book, clears his throat, and begins.

A teisho is a presentation of experiential reality (*dharma*). Ideally, it is not a conceptual discourse but an immediate demonstration of zen realization, often by way of a commentary on a koan or some other Buddhist text. The subject matter of Yamada Sensei's teisho when I entered zen was a collection of talks and letters of the fourteenth-century Japanese Rinzai Zen master Bassui, who you may recall from Chapter Six. I still remember the puzzling but deep impression these writings made on me at that time. Today I find them even deeper and more enlightening. Take for example Bassui's words "to the Abbess of Shinry uji":

> In order to become a Buddha you must discover *who* it is that wants to become a Buddha. To know this *Subject* you must right here and now probe deeply into *yourself*, inquiring: "What is it that thinks in terms of good and bad, that sees, that hears?" (Italics added)[2]

Then there is Bassui's dynamic teaching in his "Third Letter to the Zen Priest Iguchi":

> Now intensely ask yourself, "What is this which can't be named or intellectually known?" If you profoundly question, "What is it that lifts the hands, moves the legs, speaks, hears?" your reasoning will come to a halt, every avenue blocked, and you won't know which way to turn. But relentlessly continue your inquiry as to this subject. Abandon intellection and relinquish your hold on everything. When with your whole heart you long for liberation for its own sake, beyond every doubt you will become enlightened.[3]

These two passages present the very quintessence of the Rinzai Zen path. I maintain that they contain brilliant answers to the question we are discussing: Is the Ultimate personal?

Shujinko

As already mentioned in Chapter Six, Master Bassui, even as a child, began searching for the Ultimate Subject who was right there and then thinking, walking, gesturing, speaking, and hearing in his actions. This

Subject is expressed in the Japanese term *shujinko*. Bassui put his search into a very simple question: Who is the Shujinko? This term is full of profound meaning and needs unpacking.

The main meaning is contained in the two ideograms *shu* and *jin*. (*Ko* is simply added on as a term of great respect for an important person.) Both shu and jin are gender free. Thus, if the translation "master" is used, it must be read as not necessarily indicating any gender at all. Shu means main, principal, employer, master, etc. Jin is a being precisely as a person.

But what, actually, do we mean by person? Take the example of a woman who, while sleepwalking, knocks over and smashes a vase. We would not hold the sleepwalker *personally responsible* for the action, because she is not conscious at the time. True personhood demands consciousness and its consequent responsibility. Thus, I would describe a person as a conscious, responsible subject. This is exactly what is meant by shujin. So when Bassui searched for shujinko, he was seeking the great one who is the ultimate subject performing all actions. The One responsible for every act of hearing, speaking, sitting, walking, etc., of Bassui and of any and all beings.

I am reminded of the sign President Harry Truman had on his desk in the White House, "The buck stops here." Buck refers to for a buckhorn knife which used to be passed from player to player in a poker game to indicate the dealer. The dealer was responsible for his or her particular game. In the whole game of life, it is the shujinko who is responsible for everything that happens anywhere and everywhere. As we will see, it is this ultimate shujinko that zen calls our Self.

Master Rinzai (Lin-chi) is describing this shujinko when he powerfully exhorts his monks to discover the "one true person of no rank" who is the one acting whenever we do anything. Instead of shujin, he uses *shinjin*, true person, and adds the all-important point that this Ultimate Person is "of no rank"; that is, beyond all categories and therefore infinite and formless.

As a consequence of all this, one of the very best meditation practices to come out of zen is to ask yourself while sitting or walking in meditation, "Who is sitting?" "Who is walking?" This kind of searching can be continued with regard to any and all actions we do or perceive throughout our whole day. It can lead us to experience what Western mystics call "God."

The Great I AM

Finally, we find this same Ultimate Subject revealed in the Judeo-Christian tradition. Recall the great divine experience of Moses at Mount Sinai, the one which began with his seeing a burning bush which wasn't being consumed. Although his experience is reported in very anthropomorphic terms, it does present the core of Jewish mysticism—that God is doing everything. God first gives Moses a great commission: "I will send you to Pharaoh to lead my people, the Israelites, out of Egypt." (Exodus 3:10) After finally accepting this mission, Moses asks God, "But...when I go the Israelites and say to them, 'The God of your fathers has sent me to you,' if they ask me, 'What is his name?' what am I to tell them?" God replied, "This is what you shall tell the Israelites: 'I AM sent me to you.'"[4] The name I AM is written "Yahweh" in the Bible. Yahweh is the third-person form of I AM, "the One Who Is."

The message is clear. This I AM God is the subject responsible for everything that *is*. Here we have the God of Being Itself, totally universal, the subject responsible for the act of "is-ing" (be-ing) anywhere and everywhere. This revelation produced the Hebrew mysticism that experienced the voice of Yahweh in thunder and the hand of God in all wars and in peace. In Japanese zen terms, this great Person responsible for all action in the universe is the ultimate Shujinko.

Chapter 15

GOD TALK II

An empty schoolyard,
Limit and no-limit join
In the evening glow.

Return with me again to teisho time in the zendo. It is many months since I began zen and we have moved to Sanun Zendo, our own little hall beside Yamada Roshi's house that was described in Chapter Four. The teisho is over and we remain seated for the solemn recitation of the Heart Sutra. This relatively short sutra is part of the wisdom scriptures of Mahayana Buddhism. Its full title describes it as containing the very core of the great Mahayana wisdom: "The Sutra of the Heart of the Great Wisdom that Reaches the Other Shore" (in Japanese, Maka Hannya Haramita Shingyo). A more common translation for the latter part of the title is "Transcendent Wisdom." The text we are about to recite together is a seventh-century Chinese translation of the Sanskrit original, which probably dates from the fourth century.

Reality Is Bipolar

As we begin the chant, the text I am holding has the Japanese pronunciation of the Chinese ideograms given in *furigana*, phonetic symbols written beside the Chinese. However, the meaning is so difficult and my reading of even the furigana is so slow that as the group sails through the recitation it's all I can do to more or less keep up with my eyes and murmur a syllable here and there. However, one section near the beginning is so simple, clear, and repetitive that I watch for it and belt it out with the best of them. As it turns out, these four short sentences are the very heart of the Heart Sutra and have had a powerful, enlightening influence over my mind.

Shiki fu i k u.   Form is not other than Emptiness.

K u fu i shiki.   Emptiness is not other than Form.

Shiki soku ze k u.   Form *is* Emptiness.

K u soku ze shiki.   Emptiness *is* Form.

It would be useful to explain a few of the key ideograms used in this passage.

Shiki   The ideogram means color; but here it certainly has the meaning of the original Sanskrit rupa: physical shape, form, phenomenon, manifestation.

Ku   The first meaning of the ideogram is sky, precisely as empty space. Here it expresses the famous Sanskrit term sunyata, emptiness.

Fu   A negative, like not.

I   Apart from, separate, different.

Soku   An important word meaning immediate, nothing between, non-
         dual.

Ze   Has various meanings: 1. right, exact; 2. this; 3. the verb "to be."

I am well aware that there are various translations and interpretations of these lines. Mahayana Buddhism is not a monolith. There are many
nuanced understandings of both form and emptiness, especially of the latter. All that I want to do here is to expose how the understanding of these
lines that I came to has affected my whole version of reality. This effect happened regardless of whether my reading of the text squares with that of the
main line of Mahayana.

Note first that form and emptiness certainly seem to be put on
equal footing. In lines one and three, form is the subject. In two and four,
the subject is emptiness. Form is not reduced to emptiness. Rupa stands in
some kind of equality with sunyata. In his excellent book *The Heart of
Buddhist Wisdom*, Douglas A. Fox works from a Sanskrit text of the sutra.
Immediately following our four verses, the Sanskrit has a line that is not in
the Chinese version. Fox's translation of this line enforces the balance of
rupa and sunyata: "That which is form equals emptiness, and that which is
emptiness is also form."[1]

Wisdom is insight into reality. The insight given in this wisdom text
reveals that at the very heart of reality there is duality! But this cannot be
the duality of two existent beings. It's not as if you have one building block
(being) called form and another block called emptiness, which you place
side by side and then have that which we name reality. This would totally
contradict the other insight found in all wisdom teachings—that somehow
everything is one. Mahayana, above all, completely rejects a block-plus-
block dualism.

On the other hand, form and emptiness are somehow distinct and
radically opposed to each other. The word "form" certainly indicates something different from emptiness. Emptiness, in itself, surely has no form. In
fact, it is formless, without essence, beyond all categories. This analysis

teaches that existent reality is form/formless. Everything that exists is constituted of two principles of being. Existence is a bipolar coincidence of opposites. Again, neither of these two opposite poles, form or formlessness, is an existent being of itself. They are constituents of being. As opposites, they come together to constitute reality.

God Is Bipolar

Let us turn now to ultimate reality, to that which Christians call God. The term "bipolar" is especially helpful here. I was preparing a presentation for a day of Buddhist-Christian dialogue sponsored by The Center for the Pacific Rim at the University of San Francisco. While putting together some reflections on the Heart Sutra, I came across the title of a talk given by Jeffrey D. Long of University of Chicago at a recent convention of the American Academy of Religion: "Complex Ultimates: The Three-Bodied Buddha, the Two-Natured Brahman, and the Bipolar God." The words "complex ultimates" and "bipolar God" rang a bell within me. Yes! The Ultimate is complex. It is bipolar. This is just what the Heart Sutra says. It is also what the Christian doctrine of the Trinity enunciates.

I can't recall exactly when it was that I first made the connection between the formless/form teaching of Buddhism and the Father-Son doctrine of Christianity, but for years the Mahayana understanding of reality (as I grasped it) has enlightened the Trinity for me. Reflect for a moment on what Christian tradition says about the first two "Persons." The first is Father, Mother, Generator, Manifestor, the Source out of which everything arises. The second is Son, Daughter, Only Begotten, Generated, Manifestation, the Pattern (Logos) according to which everything exists. These two are clearly distinct and opposite to each other, but at the same time are one ultimate reality. As with formlessness and form, neither the First nor the Second "Person" is a self-existent being, because they join (together with the Spirit) to constitute one God, one Divine Being. Neither ever exists apart from the other. In the Christian paradigm, the ultimate is clearly a complex being, a bipolar God who exists as a coincidence of opposites.

The question, of course, arises as to the validity of identifying the Emptiness pole of the Heart Sutra with the Father and the Form pole with the Son of the Trinity. Certainly there are many things in the Buddhist and Christian analyses of reality that do not jibe. However, the two systems do come together in positing a bipolar ultimate. What is more, the basic character of these two poles is the same. At the beginning of the New Testament "Letter to the Colossians" are some profound and beautiful poetic lines. They seem to be a quotation of what was most likely an early liturgical hymn. Lines 13-14 of Chapter One have spoken of "his beloved Son." This is the subject of the relative clause that follows: "...who is the image of the invisible God, the firstborn of all of all creation. For in him were created all things in heaven and earth..." (Col. 15-16) God is here called invisible.

This is traditional Hebrew teaching. Yahweh cannot be seen; therefore, one is to use no graphic image of God. As this insight developed in Christianity under the impact of Greek philosophy, God is always affirmed as infinite, beyond all limits. But an infinite reality can have no form, because the very idea of form means shape and boundary.

God Is Infinite/Finite

We are so accustomed to the statement "God is infinite" that we don't often notice the possible confusion it contains. If you take the sentence to mean that God is *only* infinite, then how can God be triune? How can there be two, let alone three "Persons" in God? To have two, there must be some kind of difference and distinction. But if infinity is the only reality in God, how can there be any difference? There can be no boundaries in infinity to distinguish it from infinity. The opposite of formlessness cannot be formlessness. An absolutely empty sky (*k u*) has nothing to distinguish it from empty sky.

Take the example of an empty cup. It is a bipolar reality made of the cup and the emptiness. Remove the confining cup form and you don't have anything at all! To have cup emptiness you must have a form (container) that is empty. So also, there cannot be sunyata without rupa, yin without yang, negative without positive, a parent without a child. Ultimately, monopolar reality is a contradiction in terms and unreal.

Return for a moment to the lines "Shiki soku ze k u. K u soku ze shiki." Earlier I gave the usual translation of these sentences: Form *is* Emptiness. Emptiness *is* form. But this hardly brings out the force of the word soku. Take the Japanese expression *sokushi*, instant death. A person is alive; the next instant dead. There is nothing between the two states. Soku means nothing between, immediate, so immediate that when it joins two, the two constitute only one reality. To bring this out, we can translate the sentences as: Form is-es right together with Emptiness, and vice versa. They *never* exist apart. To say that God is formless must be balanced by God as form. If we say that God is infinite, we must also affirm that God is finite.

To say that the Divine is infinite, invisible, indescribable, and formless is true. But this can only be said of one pole of the bipolar God, the first "Person." If there truly are two "persons," then the second must be distinct and opposite; that is, in some sense finite, visible, describable and in form. I feel that the logic in all this is impeccable. (This presentation of the bipolar, triune God will be further refined, but for now we can let it stand as is.) This "Image of the invisible God, the firstborn of all creation" is the "Son," the Universal Form, the Logos (Pattern) according to which are "created all things in heaven and earth."

I would like to reinforce this unusual position about God by looking again at the other two sentences from the Heart Sutra which we have been considering. "Shiki fu i k u. Ku f u i shiki." They can be retranslated into: Form is not incompatible with Emptiness. Emptiness is not incompatible with Form. This translation expresses one of the great lights of my life.

For many years I have pondered over the connection between God and creatures and how it is that we can become one with God. I was brought up on the fundamental affirmation that infinite and finite are absolutely distinct. If a being is infinite, it cannot in any way be finite, and vice versa. The two are contradictory opposites. How, then, can a finite creature be one with the infinite God? What is more, how can there be a "God-man, "a divine incarnation? As I recall, one of the early shifts toward some solution of this problem came in Taiwan.

It was late one afternoon. I was staying on the campus of Sheng Kung Girls High School in Tainan, writing a book with Sr. Lee Chwen Jiuan, one of the community of Sisters who runs the large school. The students had all gone home and the whole schoolyard was empty. Tired from writing, I was walking around the quiet campus. It was then that it dawned on me. Infinity and finiteness, eternity and time, *are not incompatible*! They do not mutually exclude each other, because they are not in the same category. Large and small with regard to the same norm are incompatible because they are both in the category of size, but infinity is not in any category at all.

At the time I hardly understood all the implications of this insight. As the light grew over the years, I came to realize that the two opposites are compatible also, because they are not *existent* beings. About three years ago, I hit upon the term "constituents of being" in regard to form and emptiness and finally as to the "persons" of the Trinity.

Hypostasis

Christianity is often seen to be incurably dualistic. God and creatures, time and eternity, finite and infinite, are all taken as essentially distinct *and* incompatible. In the paradigm I am proposing, these distinctions are not as bifurcating as they seem. Just as in Buddhism, so also in Christianity there is no crass dualism at the heart of reality. Consider the word *hypostasis,* which is used in Greek Christianity when speaking about each of the three "persons" in God. *Hypo* means under; *stasis* is a standing, a stance. Each of the three divine "persons" is "one-that-stands-under," or simply a "stander-under." But together they form one god. This says, then, that none of the three hypostases is an existent being of itself. If they were, there would be three gods. They are "standers-under," not "standers-out." (The "ex" in existent means out.) The two opposites, Father and Son, come together in the Holy Spirit to constitute one existent Divinity.

God Is Three-In-One

I am sure that you have already been wondering about how the Holy Spirit fits into this paradigm of the bipolar God. From the second century on, working from the not-too-clear teachings in the scriptures, Christian theology came to teach that there are not two but three hypostases in Divine Being. The Third "Person" was said to be the union of the first Two, the principle of life and love. I would suggest that one way to discover the Holy Spirit is to reflect on the simple word "being." We seem to use this word with two very distinct nuances. When we say *a* being, it feels like a static noun, such as a chair, a car, or a TV set. However, grammatically, being is a verbal noun. It indicates action. To feel this more basic meaning of the word, try changing be-ing to is-ing. For example, the is-ing of God is bipolar. This indicates that the two poles Father and Son exist in action. This action, this movement, is what we call the Holy spirit.

In the Christian scriptures, people such as Jesus, Paul, and Barnabas are described as "led by the Spirit" or "moved by the Holy Spirit." Such expressions should not be read to mean that there is a "Person" up in heaven called Spirit who is moving people around like pieces on a chess board. Rather, the movement *itself* is the Spirit. The Source of the Movement is the First "Person" and the Second is the Pattern, the Logos, according to which the Movement happens.

This primal Movement is two way. To begin with, it is the Movement of the Formless Source into Form, into the "firstborn of all creation." This Movement *into* Form proceeds through the Logos into less universal, more exclusive and restricted forms, until it extends even into an all-exclusive, distinct-from-all-others-form which we call an individual being. A perfect example of this process is given to us in Jesus of Nazareth. He is described as having been born of the Source by the power of the Holy Spirit Movement. At about the age thirty, he came to full, mature manifestation as an individual "image of the invisible God." At this point, the movement of his life turned and the Spirit led him back to the "Father"-Source. At the beginning of John's account of the passion, death, and resurrection of Jesus, he is described as "fully aware...that he had come from God and was returning to God." The Movement we call the Spirit is both *from* the Source into form and *back to* the Source, so as to rise to a new and higher life form.

GOD AND US

The ego hates
To Hear, "Between God and you
There is no between"

I t was summer of 1982, during the Naropa Institute's conference on spirituality in Boulder, Colorado. The Taiwanese Sister Agnes Lee Chwen Jiuan was there because I had heard that she was on her way to her community's headquarters in New Jersey and suggested she stop in for the conference. Neither of us knew anyone else among the participants, so we ended up eating our lunch together each day. I had met Sister many months before in Japan and found that we had large areas of mutual interest. Our deep and fascinating conversations continued at Boulder. One thing that amazed me was her profound freedom of thought. As an Easterner, she was far more radical and free about Christian teaching and practice than I ever was. One of her remarks is still with me, "What's so wrong with Pantheism?"

All my life, especially during my long studies, nothing has been more taboo than pantheism. Any line of thought that even seemed to move toward this forbidden idea has been utterly inadmissible and promptly rejected. Yet a Chinese Catholic religious Sister was seemingly in favor of it, at least to some degree. However, deep down in myself I discovered a similar feeling. In Japan, I had grown to love the Shinto experience. After all, we have always said that God is in all things. What does this really mean? The whole goal of the Christian path is to become one with God, but how can this be? At the beginning of Chapter 14, the point was made that we creatures are *not* in relation to God as we are to each other. It's time now to delve further into the question of God and us.

Are God And Creation One or Two?

When speaking of God and creatures, we can begin with two utterly opposite and contradictory positions: *monism* and *dualism* (pluralism). This monism/dualism contrast is founded on the famous problem of the one and the many. In the West, ever since the days of the early Greeks, philosophers have struggled to find a system of thought that can account for both the obvious multiplicity in the universe and the radical oneness that enlightened ones have always experienced. As we shall see, the truth is somewhere in the middle between these two positions. The whole paradigm I am presenting is based on the coincidence of opposites.

Christianity is usually considered to be quite dualistic. It certainly accepts this universe with all its diversities as real and fully distinguishes it from the *one* God. Christian liturgical prayers are full of dualistic divisions: God/creatures, Infinite/finite, eternal/temporal, Kingdom of God/this world, Heaven/earth, good/evil, etc.

Probably the greatest and most uncompromising dualism is felt in the first two pairs of this list, God/creatures and Infinite/finite. God is usually thought of as an infinite being, while all creation is made up of finite beings, radically distinct from God. God and creation add up to two. Yet Christianity is not as unmitigatingly dualistic as it might seem. God is always spoken of as both transcendent, inasmuch as the Infinite is beyond all categories, and immanent, in that God gives being to and is actively present in all "finite" creatures. Even though the experiences of the Christian mystics are not always understood or accepted by a church limited by ordinary consciousness, they often teach that reality is an actual coincidence of the very opposites which seem so dualistic. The great Catherine of Genoa (d. 1510) finds herself and God to be one when she says that God is "my being, my self," and she speaks of love as "true transformation into God."[1]

On the other hand, Buddhist language does at times seem to be truly monistic. This world with all its multiplicity is often spoken of as an illusion, a dream. The only reality is the one "suchness" or "emptiness" experienced in enlightenment. However, as Yasutani Roshi often used to say, this "one" is not a numerical "one." Without going further into Buddhism, we can say that there are a number of thought systems which, in effect, choose the one and give no reality to the many. When this one is held to be the one God, we have monistic pantheism, in distinction from pluralistic pantheism or polytheism, in which there are many gods.

Knowing Sister Agnes Lee well, and even having co-authored a book with her, I can say that she was not talking about either kind of pantheism. She was certainly affirming that there is only one God, but that somehow we are not as distinct from God as we usually imagine. Her thought came out in an even more striking way three years later, during a Buddhist-Christian dialogue conference put on by Mercy Center. Well over a hundred people were gathered in our Sequoia Room that evening. In response to a question during her rather brief presentation, Sister said very simply, "Yes, I am God." These words were like an electric shock that immobilized the whole audience. Some people smiled, others frowned, some held their breath, and many just sat rather stunned. The great taboo had been breached! Later, one lady in great agitation said something like, "She has taken away all that we've got." This woman felt that Sr. Agnes was robbing her of the great and loving God "up there" to whom we can turn for strength, light, and peace, as to a firm rock of refuge. For her, this Father in Heaven is our only certainty in this sad, difficult, even hostile world. Of course, to rob people of their divine security was not Sister's intent at all.

Just the opposite. In her mind, we have much greater grounds for confidence and peace because we are not separate from God in such a dualistic way.

Since Sr. Agnes and I were giving a joint presentation that evening, I rushed up to the microphone to say that in the West that way of speaking could too easily be misunderstood. That it might be better to say, "We are God in manifestation." There was a special meeting the next morning to calm down the flurry Sister's remark had aroused. This only upset Sister herself, because deep down she felt she had said something that needed to be said. When she sadly spoke to me about the meeting, I basically agreed with her. For years I had been saying that we Christians do not seem to really accept the scriptural teaching about entering eternal life and sharing the divine nature. If we take these assertions seriously, we must say that in some very real sense we *are* divine. Doshin handles this matter of our divinity and the problem of pantheism in Chapter 13, but a brief review might be helpful.

The rejection of pantheism is usually built on the logic that an infinite be-ing is incompatible with a finite be-ing. If a finite be-ing were to somehow actually share in infinite be-ing, then it would no longer "be" finitely. But, as the logic goes, all creatures, including ourselves, are finite be-ings. Therefore, we cannot at the same time "be" infinitely. In such an analysis of reality, pantheism is a total contradiction and impossible. However, all this impeccable logic hinges on the truth of the following two assumptions:

1.   God is purely and only an infinite, formless be-ing.

2.   All creatures are purely and only finite, form be-ings.

If these two assumptions are true, not only is pantheism impossible, but very much more is impossible besides:

A.   Creatures cannot enter eternal life, because only infinite life is eternal.

B.   Creatures cannot share the divine (infinite) nature.

C.   We cannot actually be(come) one with God.

D.   Even statements such as "We are in God and God is in us" seem to have little reality.

Statements A through D all contain common Christian teachings based on the Bible. If we truly accept them, then we must say that neither statement 1 nor statement 2 above is valid! As we have already maintained so many times, both God and creatures are infinite/finite realities.

Consider again the remarkable assertion Paul makes in his famous address to the Athenians: "In him [God] we live and move and have our being." (Acts 17:28) Our human life happens within divine life. Every movement we creatures make is a concrete manifestation of the one movement of the Source into Form and back. Our be-ing is within the divine Be-ing and is never separate from the one Flow we call the Holy Spirit. Every step we take, every thought we have, every action of our lives is literally a divine event.

Holonic Anthropology

The best expression I know to describe our unique "relationship" to God is to say that we are *holons to the Whole*. Holon is a term created by Arthur Koestler from the Greek *holos*: whole, entire.[2] A holon is a whole, a unit, which exists within a large whole. Take for example the index finger of your left hand. There is a muscle in the front of the finger which enables it to curl down toward the palm of your hand. Start with one atom in this muscle. It is a unit unto itself, distinct and separate. Yet this one atom's very life and function is to be part of one of the molecules in the muscle, a holon in relation to the whole molecule. In the same way, each molecule is a holon within a cell, which is a holon to the muscle, which is a holon to the finger, which is a holon to the entire body. But your body is a holon to your body-mind-spirit whole, which is a holon within a very real entity called humanity.

But the process does not stop there. This "relationship" of holon to whole pervades all of creation with increasing complexity/simplicity until we reach the Ultimate Whole, the Universal Energy Form Field—God. Thus, to paraphrase Paul: In the Ultimate Whole, we human holons live and move and have our be-ing.

Two points are to be noted here. First, as we've maintained so often, our "relationship" as holons to the Ultimate Whole is not the same as that between holon and holon. Between you and me, inasmuch as we are two human holons, there is a truly dualistic relationship. We are two distinct human be-ings related in one common humanity. Holon-I do not live and move and have my be-ing in holon-you. Our be-ings are truly distinct units. On the other hand, neither of us is fully distinct from God. You and God are not two distinct beings related to each other in some commonality. God is be-ing and you "be" within God, as a holon in a whole.

Non-Dualism

This be-ing in The Be-ing is neither dualistic nor monistic. For want of a better word, we often use *non-dualistic*. (A better term might be *holonic*.) The ancient Sanskrit word for non-dualism is *advaita*. This is more correctly, but not usually, spelled *aduaita*: a-dua = a-dual = not two. The great spiritual pioneer Swami Abhishiktananda (Henri Le Saux, O.S.B) delved deeply into Hindu Vedantic aduaita. This Benedictine mystic's conclusion was:

> Advaita means precisely this: neither God alone, nor creature alone, but an indefinable non-duality which transcends at once all separation and confusion.[3]

In another place he insists:

> In reality the advaita lies at the root of Christian experience. It is simply the mystery that God and the world are not two.[4]

Since we Christians so often approach God as a separate, distinct "Great Other," we need to listen to clear words such as these to become aware of our infinite/finite reality. Just as every atom in your finger is a human atom, so every human be-ing is a divine human.

Another point to note is that the Divine Whole-human holon connection is not the same as the relationship of part to whole as this is usually understood. Take the classic example of a wrist watch. It has many parts put together to form a kind of whole, but you would never say that the whole watch is present in the minute hand, in the battery, or in any of its other parts. Yet God, the Divine Whole, is totally present in each and every human be-ing. Modern technology provides us with an extraordinarily fine phenomenon to illustrate this amazing non-dual presence of the Divine Whole in each creature holon

Holographic Presence

The term *holographic* again from the Greek *holos* (whole, entire) and *graphein* (to write). Holographic means that the whole is written in each holon. A hologram is created by a complicated process in which a non-diffusive laser beam is split into two beams. Imagine that one beam covers an apple and then proceeds off into space. The other beam is deflected to a mirror and reflected back to intersect the beam from the apple. Where the two laser beams collide, an interference field is created, similar to that created when the waves caused by two rocks thrown into a pool come together. A photographic film is then put into the interference field and photographs it. If you print out this film negative, all you get is a picture of a lot of squiggles. But if you leave the film as a negative slide and pass a laser beam through it, the original apple appears on the other side of the slide as a three-dimensional light form in beautiful color. This is a hologram.

This in itself is interesting, but it still does not show the holographic character of the apple in the interference field. The next step is to cut the slide in half. Now, take the upper half of the slide and shine the beam through it. You might expect that only the upper half of the apple would be projected. But no, a three-dimensional image of the whole apple forms! If you cut the slide into a hundred pieces and shine the light through any piece, you still get a hologram of the complete apple. The whole is "written" throughout the entire slide. The only change that occurs is that as the pieces get smaller, the image of the whole becomes progressively dimmer and fuzzier.

God is holographically present in every creature holon. The divine Be-ing is omnipresent, but not just in the sense that God is actually present in everything; the *whole* God is totally present in each holon. The parallel with a photographic hologram seems to hold even to the extent that the "smaller" and more restricted the holon is, the less radiantly clear is the Divine Presence. God is more clearly seen in an Angel then in a wayward human. Be that as it may, the holographic nature of our connection with God is a truly helpful description of what Abhishiktananda calls the "indefinable non-duality which transcends at once all separation and confusion."

At last we can appreciate Sister Agnes's statement, "Yes, I am God." Her is-ing is God's Is-ing. Her be-ing is God's Be-ing. Our ultimate self-identification is to say "Yes, I, as a holon, am God, the Whole, manifesting in this individual." From all this arise obvious implications in regard to our private and liturgical prayer in Christian circles. Somehow the pervading dualism of liturgical prayer must be corrected. Our whole lives can be changed, so that we truly do come to find God in all persons, things, and events. One of the greatest sentences I have ever read (attributed to Meister Eckhart) is: "Between God and me there is no between."

Chapter 17

THE GOD-FIELD

The cosmos in a grain,
In this one note the whole
Divine symphony.

As I sit here composing this chapter, a Vivaldi violin concerto is playing in the background. I am listening to it on KDFC, a local radio station that features classical music. There are probably thousands of people in the San Francisco Bay Area hearing this very same concerto. This simple fact may not seem like something important to write about, but the ordinary radio broadcast we take for granted is actually an amazingly illuminating event.

Energy Form Field

To begin with, a radio broadcast is a field of energy. A *field* is an area where a certain power is in action. Thus, the nature of a field is determined by the kind of power at work. A baseball field is where baseball power is actualized; that is, where a baseball game is played. A radio broadcast is an electromagnetic field. It starts with a transmitter that sends out radio waves corresponding to sound waves. These waves have a definite form. My receiver dial is set at 102.1 Megahertz on the FM radio band. This means that the basic form of KDFC's electromagnetic waves is such that the modulation of the frequency of the waves occurs 102.1 million cycles or Megahertz per second. Although this is their basic form, the waves contain many form variations within them, corresponding to the music or voice information being transmitted. The main point is that a field is created by (1) a source and (2) a movement, according to (3) a basic form. It seems that the word energy was coined by Aristotle himself. *En* here means not so much "in" as "at." *Ergy* comes from the Greek verb *ergein*, "to work." So energy is a power source at work.

This whole radio energy field is highly intelligent and, in a social sense, personal. The transmitter, the radio waves, and their form may seem totally impersonal. But the source, taken in its entirety, includes not only the intelligent persons who designed and built the transmitter, but also all the intelligences responsible for the music on the CD being played and the station personnel responsible for its choice and broadcast. This personal character of an energy field will be important when we speak of God as the Universal Energy Form Field.

As I sit here listening to KDFC (it's Mozart's Jupiter symphony now), I am hearing the *whole* of the transmission from the source. I don't hear just the violins, while listeners in Oakland hear nothing but the cellos and people in San Rafael only drums. We each hear it all. My receiver is taking in only a tiny portion of the radio waves being sent out in the KDFC field, yet I am enjoying the whole transmission. A radio field is holographic! Any small part of the waves that is caught by any radio anywhere in the field contains the whole source at work in the 102.1 Mhz form.

The Triune God

"Almighty, ever-present God, Source of all…" is an ordinary way that we might begin a Christian prayer. In less conventional but just as valid terms, we can describe God as the Universal Energy Form Field:

(1) God, as Source, is infinite energy, unlimited power at work. The power that creates this field is not confined to any category such as electromagnetic or gravitational. Divine Energy is totally universal. It is simply the power to be. Hebrew mysticism, dating from Moses at the foot of Mt. Sinai, calls God Yahweh, "The One Who Is."

(2) The movement of the Divine Source is simply be-ing. "To be" is universal, beyond all categories. But at the same time, it is always found within a category. (More on this point later.)

(3) The form of this divine movement is also universal—the Logos, the Pattern. "All things come to be through the Word." (Jn. 1:3) Note the verbal form in this statement is "come *to be*."

We are not saying by all this that God is like a field of radio energy. Rather, the triune character of a radio field—source, movement, in form—is only a particular manifestation of the Trinity holistically present in everything.

The God-Field Is A Person

To speak of God as the Universal Energy Form Field, then, is by no means to say that God is an impersonal reality. A person is an intelligent, responsible subject. The one divine "Source Moving into Form" is the all-intelligent Subject responsible for all be-ings, both actual and potential. In fact, any intelligence and subjective responsibility that we creatures have is nothing but the Divine Intelligent Subject manifesting in our personhood, the divine Person individualized.

To call God an almighty Force Field, then, is not to set the divine in opposition to ourselves as weak, limited creatures. Rather, it is to unveil the ultimate foundation of our existence. It does not separate us from God, but reveals us as holons in the Divine Whole. We often speak of God as both transcendent to all creatures and as immanent in all. However, the anonymous *Cloud Of Unknowing*, a profound fourteenth-century text on Christian contemplation, teaches that God is neither outside us nor inside us. God simply is. When we remain at the level of our ordinary categorizing intellect, we cannot help but speak of God as outside and/or inside. But in reality, God simply *is*.

"God's Arms"

The old-time comedian Joe E. Brown had a striking experience of this all-knowing, all-loving Personal Energy Field. It was during World War II. He had just heard of the death of his son Don, a pilot. He writes:

> The next few days were a dark abyss. I seemed to be falling through endless chaos. I *couldn't get hold of myself*. And then one night when I was alone, I felt something I had never known before. It was the presence of God. It was a peace that passes understanding. I felt God's arms around me, in a way I cannot possibly describe.[1] (Italics added)

The shock of his loss had torn him out of the ordinary world and away from his usual little-local-self-consciousness. Vulnerable and sensitive, he broke through to the hidden dimension of our be-ing which we call love. He felt God as loving because all reality is one divine flow. To discover oneness is to find love. In the same book, Brown sums up his life experience in the beautiful words, "Just remember that everything that happens to you is pure velvet."[2] Everything that happens is a personal act of God!

God As Power At Work

I am seated in a beautiful redwood-paneled room of the faculty building at our former Jesuit theologate in Alma, California. A board of four Jesuit examiners is asking me questions that range over seven years of philosophical and theological studies. The format of my presentation and of their questions is the centuries-old thesis-proof-objections-answers method of scholasticism. This grand oral exam goes on for two long hours...all in Latin. As I look back now, there is no question that these many years of Jesuit education had a profound and beneficial influence on my life.

Due to this intellectual training, one of the models of reality that became basic in all my mental work was and still is that of *potency and act*. Our primary teaching source during those seven years was Thomas

Aquinas, the great intellect and saint, who used the physics and philosophy of Aristotle as a basis for his immensely influential theological synthesis. In many chapters of this book, I have been using Aristotelian/Thomistic categories. Here we can employ the potency-act analysis of reality both to review and to advance our insight into the paradigm I have been presenting about God. The following may seem too abstract at times and hardly more than dead intellectualism, but give it a try. The outcome could surprise you.

Potency and act is a simple and fundamental analysis of reality. For example, you have just started your car. While the engine is idling, it has the power to move the car. It is in potency to move. When you put the motor into gear and the car moves, this is potency in act. So we have the power *to* act (while idling) and the power *in* act (while moving). When St. Thomas applied these ideas to God, he maintained that God is infinite-power-*in*-act. This is certainly true in the ordinary Western model of reality, because God is said to be infinite be-ing. In such a position, the power-*to*-act is denied to God. On the other hand, what we have maintained all along is that in the Divinity there are both infinite-formless and finite-form poles.

Focus for a moment on the infinite pole, the formless constituent of reality. When this pole is in existence, it is quite true to say that this pole is infinite power-in-act. It is perfect. It is always at fullness. When people discover this aspect of reality in a wonderful enlightenment experience, they are overjoyed. It's true, everything is perfect! For years, when speaking about our actual world, I have said, "Yes, things may be a mess, but they are a perfect mess!" A broken cup is a manifestation of pure, perfect, total act. Suzuki Shunryu Roshi of the San Francisco Zen Center used to say, "Everything is perfect, but there is a lot of room for improvement."

A Repetition And Beyond

Return for a moment to the model in which God is *only* infinite act. When this purely infinite be-ing creates, where does finite be-ing come from? How can being-in-form arise out of nothing but formlessness? If you hold that the whole world of form is pure illusion, you have no problem. There is only boundless power in formless act. But there also is no Trinity, no diversity, no creation at all. On the other hand, if you accept the world of form as real (and both Buddhism and Christianity do in rather different ways), you must face the question, Where does form come from?

One of the Latin sayings we always used in our studies was *nemo dat guod non habet* (no one gives what one does not have). This is true even of God as source. God must be in form potentially in order to create form. The Divine Potency (the Source, the Father/Mother God) is both formless and an unlimited number of potential forms. The Divine Movement (the Spirit) is also formless and in form. The Divine Potency in Act (the Son), too, is formless and in actual form. So we have come again to the heart of reality—the coincidence of opposites. The two opposing elements, formless and form, are together in each of the Three Constituents. At the infinite pole alone, there can be no change. Because of the finite pole, there is constant evolutionary change.

The first of all models of reality in recorded history is that of the *I Jing* (or *I Ching*). The insights of this system are amazingly profound and still fresh. Its oldest stratum probably goes back to the twelfth century B.C.E.. It, too, is bipolar (yin and yang), with one movement, which forms a trinity. The very name of the document, *A Treatise On Change*, indicates its experiential origins.

God In Process

Today there is but one religious dogma in debate: What do you mean by "God"? In this respect, today is like all yesterdays. This is the fundamental religious dogma, and all other dogmas are subsidiary to it.

Alfred N. Whitehead [3]

The scientist Alfred N. Whitehead was led by his mathematical insights into a groundbreaking investigation into philosophy and religion. It was the ideas of Whitehead that gave impetus to a new theological development called process theology. During the nine months I spent at the

School of Applied Theology in Berkeley, California, there was a curriculum segment on process theology. At the time, almost seventeen years ago, I couldn't make head or tail out of the professor's classes. The ideas were confusing. That there could be change in God was quite contrary to the infinite, eternally unchangeable God I had learned about. However, my curiosity was aroused and the ideas stayed with me.

Richard McBrien, when reporting this theological movement in his book *Catholicism*, puts its position very clearly: "...[It] understands God and all reality as a constant 'process' of change and movement forward—nothing is fixed or immutable..."[4] For years, I have been deeply impressed by the Taoist analysis of reality as a dynamic movement. The ideogram *Tao* basically indicates a movement, a flow. These ideas mesh perfectly with process thought. It finally all came together for me when I discovered the etymological meaning of the word creation.

Ker is the Indo-European root of the verb create. Its basic meaning is "to grow." Crescent, increase, and create are all formed from this root; Ceres (Keres) is the goddess of agriculture, of growing. When we call God the Creator, what do we mean? Does God increase in the act of creating? Or does it mean that God remains exactly the same, while all growth is strictly outside God? Here the ideas we have developed about the finite pole of divine reality can be illuminating. The Divine Source, precisely as unlimited potency to be in form, has the built-in drive to exist in form more and more. Creator means grower!

The Source-Movement-Form God is by nature creative and crescent. Increase is the very law of life. Jesus said, "I have come that you may have life and have it *more abundantly*." (Jn. 10:10) In his own life cycle, he showed us the pattern of all life: birth-growth-maturity-decline-death-new life. Be-ing arises from the Source, moves through the Universal Form (the Logos) into less universal archetypal form and into individual forms, matures, dies to that limited and completed form, and returns to the "Increaser" Source so as to rise to increased be-ing. The potency is unlimited, so the act can go on and on, evolving into greater act. We live in an ever-expanding universe. Finally, recall that all creatures are holons within the Whole. God and creation are not two separate be-ings. If creation is in process, then God is in process, because God is the Ultimate Subject responsible for all that happens, including change.

I hope that these ideas about God as Universal Form Field, as Creator, and as in Process, have not seemed out of your world and unconnected with your needs. Actually, they are the basis for profound intimacy and oneness. As a creature, as a holon within the Whole, you exist within the embrace of an inexpressibly wonderful Person who wills nothing but ever-increasing knowledge, love, and life for you in *every* event of your life. Nothing that you do can ever separate you from this infinitely/finitely loving Be-ing. You live and move and have your being in divine light, divine strength, clarity, love, and patient perfection. Separation can only happen in your awareness, not in your reality. We are often confused, weak, hurting, and hurtful, because we are not aware of who and what we are. So we remain on pilgrimage. We still acutely feel the need to be saved from our blindness and all that it brings. It is time, then, to move on to Christ and our salvation.

Chapter 18

HOLONIC CHRISTOLOGY

*To "I am the Light
Of the world." Jesus adds,
"You are, too."*

T he scene again is the little Sanun Zendo in Kamakura. I am sitting there struggling to quiet my mind and imagination so I can focus on MU. Although there are a number of foreign Christians and even some Japanese Christians in the zendo, nobody is thinking, let alone talking, about Jesus. There's not a Christian image in sight, and the bows we make are to Buddhist statues and to our zen roshi. I strongly feel that zazen will make me a better Christian, yet here I am spending the whole time without any thought at all about Jesus or any devotion to him. Coming out of a life-long devotion to Jesus Christ, I am sitting in the zendo as a Christian, but clearly remember asking myself: Were is Christ in all this?

The answer, too, is still with me: True, I'm not thinking about him, not showing any devotion to him, but what I am doing is be-ing Christ. At the time, I wasn't too clear what I meant by this, but it did satisfy. After years of reflection, I can further explicate the meaning of "be-ing Christ."

Jesus for the Twenty-First Century

We start with the *human* be-ing of Jesus. I have no question at all about his divinity, but this is because, in general, I do not radically distinguish humanity and divinity in the way they have been separated so long in Christian tradition. The huge effort made by both Greek and Roman theologians to prove the divinity of Jesus has often, in effect, obscured his humanity. Also, Jesus has been so exalted and glorified by Christian piety down through the ages that sometimes his human life became rather unreal. It was more of a play put on than a real-life drama. The human need for a perfect hero and savior tends to deify Jesus so much that he is almost removed from the realm of mere mortals. In fact, most Christians would roundly deny that Jesus is a mere mortal. So I'd say we might best start by looking at Jesus as a fully realized human being.

A Questionable Christology

In this investigation, we will use not the theology that has held sway from the conciliar ages (around 300 B.C.E. on) right up to the present, but rather a new paradigm which I have come to call "holonic Christology." As we've already seen so often, the basic assumption in western Christian theology is that God is purely and simply an infinite being. There is absolutely nothing finite, nothing changing about God. On the other hand, humans are irrevocably finite, changeable beings. The question, then, about the incarnation of God is how these two beings can join in one be-ing—namely, Jesus.

It is a veritable contradiction, a huge mystery. The solution worked out was to affirm that the one Person, the Word, the Son of God and son of Mary, has two natures, divine and human. Jesus, therefore, has both divine and human consciousness and also two corresponding wills. The theory goes on to insist that these powers do not create two persons within him.

This solution seems rather neat, but it is fraught with all kinds of puzzlements. We can only touch upon a few. The infant Jesus, in his human nature, is barely conscious—as befits, say, a five-month-old baby. But at the same time, this *one person* is said to be consciously ruling the world. He is joining the Father and the Holy Spirit in creating and sustaining all creation. The logic of such ideas is correct within the system, but they have always felt strange and unreal to me.

What is more, this God/man Jesus is absolutely unique. Jesus is said to be the model of and our way to union with God. But no other human has ever been united to God in such a way! Jesus is a human being with no human personhood, even though he has a human nature. He is the *only begotten* Son of the Father. "Only" means that he is utterly unique. Only *he* is "begotten", *we* are all "made." And the name Jesus does not refer to a mere mortal person at all, but exclusively to the second of the three divine Persons, who has assumed a human nature as his own.

Add to this the underlying problem of "person." Theologically, we still do not really know what a Trinitarian person is! The result is that the whole traditional theology of the incarnation is on shaky ground. We end up simply declaring it to be a mystery. All of this was the theological background for my life until contact with Eastern insights began to throw new light on the mysteries.

A New Christology

Thus, even I was startled by what came to my lips one day during the 1982 Naropa Conference mentioned in Chapter 16. One afternoon, we ordinary participants were given an opportunity to meet the main speakers and panelists. I was especially happy to meet Brother David Steindal-Rast, O.S.B. We chatted for only a brief time, but I remember hearing myself declare that all of us are just as much the Son of God as Jesus is! The only—albeit huge—difference is that Jesus knew who he was, whereas we do not. This seemed directly contrary to the doctrine of the only begotten Son of

God. Perhaps the courage to say this was engendered by my long conversations with Sister Agnes at the conference, but I feel that already the basic assumptions of my theology had shifted because of intimate contact with Buddhism, especially its teaching about the Self/self.

Recall again the search Bassui put me on from my earliest days in zen. Who is sitting? Who is the Subject walking? Writing? Reading? We were exhorted to find a Universal Self who is the Subject ultimately responsible for everything the little local, individual self is doing. In this context, the words self and subject both indicate a person. The individual self and the Universal Self are not absolutely separate; they are only distinguished as holon and whole. An individual person is a holon of the Whole Person, God. Every "human" person is God actively manifesting as an individual. When a little-self person is perfectly righteous without any local-self-centered activity, the True Self/self reality shines out for all to see. This is what the disciples saw in Jesus, so they declared this human be-ing "My Lord and my God."

Another huge shift in my basic assumptions came out of the Buddhist teaching on Emptiness and Form as the bipolar constituents of reality. This led me to see the all-embracing importance of the intuitions of the mystics about the coincidence of opposites. There are a number of opposites, all intimately related; the most basic are infinite/finite and formless/form. Again, the coincidence of these is found in all reality, including the divine reality itself. God is, as we have repeated ad nauseam, bipolar: infinite/finite, formless/form.

If you accept this, the "mystery of the incarnation" is no longer a contradiction. Jesus of Nazareth is simply an individual manifestation of Reality Itself. His human nature is a holon within the divine nature. And this is true of all humans. Jesus was not unique in this. He was, though, special in the impeccable way his human holonic nature lived within Whole Divine Nature. When he says, "I and the Father are one," he is speaking as a holon at one with the Source in the whole. Because of his actual divine/human nature, his life is at once eternal/temporal, unborn/born, universal/particular, one/many. The Nazarene is a flawless hologram of God, of Reality Itself.

A New Anthropology

All that is said here about the person and nature of Jesus must also be claimed for every human being. The immense difference between Jesus and us is only that we are not experientially aware of ourselves and consequently do not live our lives in accord with our glorious reality. The Christian religion began when the first disciples became aware of *themselves* through their experience of Jesus, The Human Holon.

If you follow traditional theology, you can rightfully object that all this is contrary to the creedal position that Jesus is *the* unique and only begotten Son of God. It is contrary, too, to the Pauline expression that we are adopted, not natural, children of God. In response, I acknowledge that I *am* proposing a new theology here. In this new paradigm, there is only one child begotten of the Source—the totally universal Form, the Word, the second constituent of the complex Ultimate. There are not two such universal Forms, so "the Son" *is* the unique and only begotten. But every creature is this one Universal Form individualized! Thus the creedal words "only begotten" are an all-inclusive expression, not at all uniquely exclusive to Jesus of Nazareth. Jesus is truly divine and truly human, but so are you and I and every creature—all at varying levels of manifestation. We are all holons of the One Whole.

A Perfect Human Holon

In *A Brief History Of Everything*, Ken Wilber presents a long list of drives that are inherent in a holon. To further investigate the be-ing of Jesus, we will take up only the four that seem most basic. Wilber begins by saying that holons emerge, dissolve, and re-emerge inexhaustibly. Holons are always in evolutionary process. It is within this context that he discerns four essential movements or drives. Using these four, it is easy to see what a perfect human holon Jesus is and to what we are all called.

The first drive is that each holon has an obvious need to be a unit, a whole within the Whole. This is the urge to be oneself, to grow fully as a subject responsible for one's be-ing. Self-realization is a basic drive which permeates every level of holonic being because it is the very nature of the Whole Be-ing. God is "in order to" be God. A holon exists "in order to" fully be a holon. In Jesus, we have a shining example of a human holon who "advanced in wisdom, age, and grace" (Lk. 2:52) until he reached full and true holonic maturity around the age of thirty. He was then ready for evolution to a higher level of manifestation.

Integration

The second drive is to find one's place within the whole. A holon wants not just to be, but to "inter-be" (using Thich Nhat Hanh's beautiful expression) [1] and to "intra-be." It is the drive to join with all other holons to be as one Whole. This movement, too, is perfectly exemplified in Jesus. The ideal which he not only taught but also lived consistently was unconditional love of neighbor and love of God. He pointed out that this, too, is God's very nature; therefore, we who are of God have the same drive to love others as our very selves in God. "Be perfect as your heavenly Father is perfect." (Mt. 5:48) He died for the sake of all people, rose, and is now with us all days.

If the first movement is to self-realization, the second is to Self-realization. To find one's self within the Whole is to find a much vaster Self than the individual of the first drive. The small-self-identification excludes all other people and things. Universal-Self-identification is all-inclusive of every human be-ing that ever was, is, or will be. It is inclusive, too, of every creature great and small. We are, each one, holograms of the Whole. God is our very be-ing, just as in the example where the whole apple is the be-ing of each segment of the holographic slide.

Jesus realized Universal Self perfectly. He identified his own human be-ing as including all people. When Saul on the Damascus road asked Jesus for his identity ("Who are you, Lord?"), Jesus revealed his Self as including the Christians Paul was persecuting ("I am Jesus whom you are persecuting."). The first-person pronouns used by Jesus are of supreme importance. In fact, the only way to read the Gospels as they were written is to take these pronouns as expressing all-inclusive Self-identity. Whenever Jesus says I, me, my, or mine, he is speaking out of profound enlightenment. Take the example of his injunction "Follow me." If we read this "me" to indicate Jesus only in his individuality as a male Jew of the first century, then the invitation means very little and is virtually impossible to follow. No woman could "put on Christ," and the words would only make sense for first-century Hebrews. In fact, the expression sounds like megalomania. However, when we realize that this "me" refers to Jesus precisely as the Whole manifesting perfectly, then it becomes an invitation to follow him into that all-inclusive Self-identification which is the essential drive of each of us as holons. The personal pronouns of Jesus are, in effect, the Christian path to God. As Jesus said, "*I* am the way."

The third drive is to progressively evolve. Wilber calls it the urge to self-transcendence. This, again, is nothing but a divine drive. God cannot help creating. In Reality Itself there is an intrinsic necessity to create, to increase manifestation. The old Latin phrase *bonum est diffusivum sui* (good is diffusive of itself) is still valid. The source is precisely the *Source*. As a manifestation of the Source Jesus said, "I came that they may have life, and have it more abundantly." (Jn. 10:10) He accomplished this drive himself by rising to a new life, and in this very action draws us all to a whole new greater level of manifestation of the one Life.

However, the third drive can only unfold if we give up the limitations of our present way of be-ing. Thus the third drive supposes the fourth drive: self-dissolution. The new and higher can only emerge if the restricted present state literally falls apart. We must die to the old so as to rise as new. This, of course, is the paschal pattern. That Jesus in his pascha (passing over) followed this pattern perfectly is so well known to us that no further discussion seems needed. In fact, the last two holonic drives lead us right into the subject of how Jesus, by fulfilling these two movements impeccably, accomplished *our* salvation as well.

Chapter 19

JESUS' OWN SALVATION

Rising from the River,
Ascending from the Hill, the Christ
Is born anew.

I
n 1975, I flew to Cologne to direct a group of ten Japanese Sisters in a ten-day retreat. Because I was given a full-fare ticket, on the way back to Japan I was able to visit Lourdes, Munich, Jerusalem, Nepal, and Bangkok. While staying with a Jesuit classmate in Katmandu, I joined a bus tour to a major temple in honor of the Hindu goddess Kali. It was there for the first and only time in my life that I witnessed animal sacrifice. Of course, even as a child I had seen pictures of the Jewish paschal sacrifices in Bible history books, but this was my first encounter with the actual practice. What a shock! Accustomed as I was to the usual cleanliness of Japanese Buddhist temples, I couldn't help feeling uncomfortable with the messy state of the buildings and grounds in southern Nepal. But this was nothing compared to the revulsion I felt at the bloody sacrifice of that chicken.

On arrival, I saw people roasting and eating the meat of a sacrificial goat. Then at one small courtyard surrounded by Hindu statues, a mother and small daughter came in and presented a live chicken to a rather shabbily dressed priest. In a short ceremony, he prayed and then slit the throat of the poor bird with a large knife. As the blood gushed out, he quickly made the round of the statues in the courtyard, pouring the blood over them, mainly on their feet.

The picture of this blood sacrifice has never faded from my memory. I certainly empathize with the pious prayers and desires of the mother and her child. This primitive practice was all they knew and had. But as to the act itself, all I could keep saying was, "How awful. I am so glad that we don't have such rites in Christianity."

Upon reflection, though, it would seem that Christians are usually taught that our very salvation itself was, in some real sense, accomplished by a blood sacrifice—not of an animal, but of the human be-ing of Jesus Christ himself. Ever since that day in Nepal, the idea of being "redeemed by the blood of the Lamb" has been a source of increasing discomfort for me. The visual experience of such a primitive bloodletting rite has cast a whole new light on the scriptures and the theology of salvation.

I sincerely feel that we must make a penetrating reappraisal of such concepts as redemption, atonement, propitiation, and expiation. Modern scriptural scholarship and advanced anthropology can assist us to a much-needed development of salvation theology. I present some ideas along this line in the next chapter. Here, we will move on to investigate the essence of what Jesus did as savior, using both Christian tradition and insights from Eastern spirituality and modern science.

Holonic Soteriology

Soteriology, the Greek-based term for the theology of salvation, comes from the verb *sozein*, to save, to make safe. This leads us to the question with which salvation theology usually begins: What are we saved from? Basically, the scriptural answer to this question is very simple. We are saved from sin and its punishment. Although I now see this to be only a partial answer, we will go along with it for now and move to the next obvious question: What is sin? The answer we give to this will for the most part determine the kind of soteriology we end up with. For example, if sin is seen as an offense to an angry God, then our theology will be dominated by expiation, propitiation, and atonement.

Sin

In both the Jewish and the Christian scriptures, the root meaning of sin is error, failure, being off the mark. This is the basic meaning of both *hamartia*, the Greek word for sin, and *het'* or *halla't*, the interrelated words which are the most common Hebrew terms. To sin is to go off the mark, to stray from the path of righteousness. The notion of an offense to an angry God is not present anywhere in these words themselves.

To be off the mark means that we have diverted the flow of our lives into a path that is opposed to the true nature of our be-ing. We are created to be the very Flow from the Source manifesting as human individuals. We are process be-ings, nothing but energy, which means that in our very be-ing the Power Source is "at work." To be saved from being off the mark is to be drawn back into being the Reign of God in human form. The scriptures often describe salvation as a "justification," getting lined up just right. (Think of the process of justification on a word processor.) Our ideal is to be just on target, a right-on person.

Salvation

To these ideas must be joined the fundamental meaning of the Latin-based word salvation. Its root is the Indo-European word *sol*, meaning whole, complete. (Sol is the root of such words as solid, consolidated, solemn, catholic, and whole.) In holonic terms, being saved is to fully take our place as holons in the whole. We holons are only "whole"—that is, saved—when we are living in the whole. God, the Whole, is a Process in which the Source moves into Manifestation and in which the manifestation returns to the Source so as to rise to more perfect expression of the Whole. This spiraling movement is the Spirit, the Flow.

Salvation, then, consists in rejecting all thought and action that is contrary to the true Flow of be-ing. When all our thoughts, imaginings, emotions, words, and actions are nothing but the Divine Process manifesting, then we are right on the mark. We are, to use the scriptural terms, righteous and just persons. No longer in error, we are saved.

Jesus' Own Salvation

There is an even more fundamental answer to the question, what are we saved from? It is an answer that arises not out of our waywardness (sinfulness) but out of the very nature of creation itself. Remember that etymologically "to create" and "to be created" both mean *to increase*. The law of creation is that we move into a certain way of be-ing and then move on to higher and more be-ing. Life on this planet, glorious as it is, is confined and restricted. We all need to be saved from the limits of our present life. In this sense, the individual Jesus, too, had to be saved. Christians hold that Jesus of Nazareth was not guilty of sin, so he did not need liberation from sin. But even more fundamentally, as the "image of the invisible God," he was born to manifest the divine nature precisely. Inasmuch as God is Creator, the One Who Increases is "the first-born" of all creation, the archetypal model of manifestation God through the increase of life. To be whole (saved) means to actually manifest the Increasing Whole more and more perfectly in one's very be-ing.

The *only* way to more life is through death to the limitations of one's present life. Because of his own drive for more wholeness, Jesus was led by the Spirit to die to the restrictions of his earthly life and thus pass on to a new and expanded way of be-ing. There are three main restrictions: time, place, and ignorance. Ignorance consists of not seeing Reality fully. Jesus, like any human, had to move out of ignorance. In his gospel Luke says, "Jesus, for his part, progressed steadily in wisdom and age and grace before God and men." (Lk. 2:52) At his baptism by John, he advanced to an incomparable degree of enlightenment. This event at the Jordan resulted in an extremely high level of holonic integration.

The First Baptism

There beside the river, Jesus became intensely aware that he was *born of God* ("You are my beloved Son." (Mk. 1:11). Then during the scriptural period of forty days in the desert, his whole being was integrated into this baptismal insight. During that time, every action of his body, every thought, imagining, emotion, and aspiration of his psyche came to be "born of God." In zen terms, this was the *daigo tettei* of Jesus, his "great, definitive enlightenment." In Christian terms, from that time on his whole life was the Reign of God manifesting.

It is important to stress here that Jesus' baptism in the Jordan was primarily an interior event. True, it was a baptism of both body and soul. There was an important exterior element, the plunging into the Jordan and the physical sojourn in the desert. But without the inner movement of mind and spirit, these events mean little.

Besides advancing out of ignorance, Jesus, for an earth dweller, also overcame to a high degree the restrictions of time and space. As a result, he was a great psychic. In fact, one major psychic ability is to break the ordinary limits of time and place. For example, a mother who, even vaguely, knows ahead of *time* what will happen to her child who lives in a distant *place* is manifesting psychic powers. Jesus is clearly depicted as having such ability to a high degree. "'How do you know me?' Nathanael asked him. 'Before Philip called you,' Jesus answered, 'I saw you under the fig tree.'" (Jn. 1:48) A number of times he also predicted in detail the circumstances of his death on Calvary.

But such an expansion of human life was very little, compared to what Jesus certainly intuited would be his in his resurrected life. As his public life continued, Jesus felt increasingly confined. Toward the end of this life he cried out, "I have a baptism with which I must be baptized and how I am constrained until it is accomplished." (Lk. 12:50) He felt the narrow confinements of ordinary earthly life and knew that it was time to rise to greater freedom and to a more perfect individuation of the One Flow, the Spirit. He longed for a new and more profoundly transforming plunge (baptism) into Reality. What drew him to Jerusalem was the prospect of his second baptism.

The passion, death, and resurrection of Jesus of Nazareth were the climax of his own salvation process. They were the perfect fulfillment of the third and fourth holonic drives—transformation through self-dissolution. Again, we must stress the point that physical suffering and the actual shedding of blood were not the primary elements in the salvific experience of Jesus. Calvary was the place where he went to the Father. He returned to the Source to receive new and higher life. But this happened above all in his mind, will, and soul. His physical death was, in practical terms, an essential part of the process, but it did not have to be a death in which his blood was shed. Blood sacrifice is not the only way salvific death can be accomplished. It is true that we are "saved by the blood of Jesus." But these words only mean that blood sacrifice was the way he chose to manifest his interior return to the Father/Source.

What were essential were his physical death and interior sacrifice. He could have chosen some other way of dying, but blood sacrifice was still the custom in those days, so he embraced that for the physical component of his definitive rite of passage. It is striking that the most Hebrew of all the Christian scriptures, the Letter to the Hebrews, stresses this interior character of Jesus' salvific action.

> In the days when he was in the flesh [limited earthly life], he offered prayers and supplications with loud cries and tears to God, who was able to save him from death, and he was heard *because of his reverence.* Son though he was, he *learned obedience* from what he suffered; and when perfected, he became the source of eternal salvation for all who obey him. (Heb. 5:7–9; italics added)

Granted that Jesus did go through a salvation process, the question remains as to how the death and resurrection of the human individual Jesus became the "source of salvation for many." Paul says, "since one died for all, all died." (2 Cor. 5:14) What does this mean? Each of us, as an individual holon, must undergo our own self-dissolution and subsequent transformation. How can another person be said to do this for us? Before taking up this problem, we must clear away certain negative ideas about salvation that are still prevalent among Christians today.

Chapter 20

AN OUTMODED
SOTERIOLOGY

How hard it is
To believe, to stop saying
"I'm not worthy."

Before developing what our new paradigm says about salvation, it will be helpful to state clearly the punitive form of soteriology that it strongly rejects. Although this form has been in Christian circles for many centuries, it turns out to be contrary to the Scriptures and even demeaning to both God and humanity.

An Exclusivist Soteriology

The Hachiman Shrine, one of the most famous Shinto shrines in all Japan, is located in the heart of Kamakura, the city where I lived for almost seventeen years. I walked or rode down Wakamiyaoji, the cherry tree avenue leading to the shrine, more times than I can count. During the first three days of each New Year, about a million-and-a-half Japanese make their way up this avenue to perform a *hatsumode*, the first visit of the year to a shrine. I have made my own hatsumode to Shinto Shrines, Buddhist temples, and Christian churches all over Japan. In some ways it seems like just a social custom, but at the same time it is clearly a religious act. For some people the religious element is extremely shallow, whereas for others it is deep and real.

At New Year's time, passing near Hachiman-San, (a familiar way of referring to the great shrine), I often saw a sign, usually block letters on a white board, proclaiming to all the worshipers that only Jesus Christ saves. The sign was simply fixed in the ground at a strategic place or held by some zealous Christians. To me, there has always been something wrong with such a presentation of the gospel—not only because of its impoliteness and very un-Japanese-like lack of sensitivity, but even more because of the narrow, rigid teaching on salvation that it represents. In fact, I would say that it is precisely because of this kind of sectarian teaching that so few Japanese have become Christian. For well over a century, Christian missionaries of all kinds have been freely evangelizing in Japan, yet today less than one percent of the population is listed on church membership rolls.

What are we to say of the other 99 percent (amounting to nearly 125 million people)? How do they stand in relation to salvation? Are they actually all doomed to hell? Even short-time visitors to Japan meet truly good and wonderful people everywhere. To say that these millions and millions of people are not living their lives in the Flow of the Divine Spirit is not only ridiculous but also appallingly bad soteriology. The same must be said of the billions of other gracious and good non-Christians all around the world.

It is time to look more closely at the problems inherent in much of the salvation theology still taught in Christian circles. It is imperative that soteriology move out from the Christian ghetto mentality. What is needed is a theology of salvation that is compatible with the immense religious diversity and pluralism of the global village. Rahner's ideas, capsulated in his phrase, "anonymous Christians," are certainly a step in the right direction. In this and the next two chapters, we will use the questions connected with the literalist, "only Jesus saves" theology as a springboard to launch in more detail the model I call *holonic soteriology*.

Left Behind is a recent novel about life on earth after the "rapture," the event in which Jesus Christ is said to take millions of people directly into heaven without death. One of the main characters in the book is Bruce, an assistant at a rather fundamentalist Christian church. He explains to another person who was "left behind":

> "The Bible says that it's not by works of righteousness that we have done, but by his mercy God saved us. It also says that we are saved by grace through Christ, not of ourselves, so we can't brag about our goodness. Jesus took our sins and paid the penalty for them so we wouldn't have to. The payment is death, and he died in our place because he loved us. When we tell Christ that we acknowledge ourselves as sinners and lost, and receive his gift of salvation, he saves us."[1]

Not Biblical

""The Bible says...". Bruce's explanation of salvation is based on the words of the Bible taken in a very literal way. It is true that the New Testament does have expressions such as "you were ransomed...with the precious blood of Christ, like that of a lamb..." (I Peter 1:18) Words such as atonement, propitiation, and redemption are also found in the Bible. They clearly come out of a religious milieu of blood sacrifice to appease an angry God. In a way, it is too bad that they were not left behind with that culture rather than carried over into our religion, in which blood sacrifice is no longer practiced.

Even by the time the New Testament was written, these fearful words had lost their primitive meanings. Their literal meanings had disappeared and they were used in a far more sophisticated way. Modern scriptural scholars point out that these key words are subtle metaphors and not to be taken literally.

In the chapter "The Atonement Wrought by Christ" in his book *An Introduction to the Theology of the Testament*, Alan Richardson begins by saying, "The word 'Atonement' is scarcely a NT word at all."[2] He also points out that, although expressions such as "to redeem" and "to pay ransom" are not infrequent, Jesus himself is never called "redeemer" in the whole New Testament. Richardson strongly maintains that the literal interpretation and over-emphasis of such terms as redemption, propitiation, lamb of God, etc., has done great theological harm.

Toward the end of the chapter, he points out that the satisfaction theory of salvation—which, sad to say. is part of Christian tradition—is not actually biblical. This means that it is not appropriate to introduce this literalist, fundamentalist soteriology with "The Bible says," and certainly not as "the New Testament says." Richardson writes:

> The NT writers certainly regard Is. 53, as Jesus had done before them, as predicting the sacrificial death of Christ, but they do not use it to teach a 'substitutionary' or a 'satisfaction' theory of the atonement. The curious notion that 'God's Justice,' which demands the punishment of sinners, could be saved by inflicting the death penalty upon the one sinless being who had ever lived on earth, is not found in the NT and it should find no place in Christian theology.

> As we have noted above, the metaphors of redemption and ransom are not intended by the NT writers to suggest that a price has been paid either to God or to the Devil; the metaphor emphasizes the length to which God is prepared to go for man's salvation, the sacrifice which Christ was willing to make.

> Medieval conceptions of God as a kind of feudal overlord who requires satisfaction for his outraged honour have no

place in a genuinely biblical theology; and post-Reformation notions of Christ's bearing a penalty or punishment instead of us, in order that God might forgive us and yet remain just, have no basis in the teaching of the NT.[3]

In the text quoted from *Left Behind*, Bruce says, "Jesus took our sins and paid the penalty for them so we wouldn't have to. *The payment is death*, and he died in our place because he loved us." (Italics added) Besides its shaky biblical foundation, there are other serious difficulties with Bruce's theology. If we accept it as stated, it implies some very unpleasant things, both about ourselves and about God. God comes across as constantly offended and as demanding a huge penalty for human offences. In the primitive anthropomorphic imagery of some scriptures, God is even portrayed as angry and vengeful. "Vengeance is mine, saith the Lord," can be read this way.

Fear and Guilt-Ridden

St. Anselm, theologizing along these lines in the eleventh century, taught this punitive theology of salvation in a powerful way. He said that the magnitude of an offense is determined by the dignity of the one offended. God's dignity is infinite, so our offences are infinite. But we are only finite creatures (there's that supposition again), so we can never offer adequate satisfaction or expiation for any of our sins. God, then, in "his" merciful love, sent the Divine Son to offer a sacrifice of atonement in our place. Since the Son is of infinite dignity, our salvation is finally accomplished. In this model, God is a kind and loving father, but at the same time is a just judge who sees sinners as infinitely offensive and must demand complete expiation.

What does this punitive paradigm of salvation tell us about humans, about ourselves? Perhaps the best way of answering this is by looking at how these literalist teachings have actually impacted the lives of Christians. Many good Christians have basically lived their lives in fear of God and with an ever-present, all-pervading sense of guilt. Christians have been taught to think and even love to sing about the amazing grace shown to "a wretch like me." In this fear-ridden and guilt-ridden psychology, our *real* self is thought and felt to be weak, always sinning, helpless, born in sin, and estranged from God. Our only hope is in *supernatural* graces from God bought by the penalty-paying blood of Jesus.

Such abusive human self-identity reached a kind of climax in the Calvinist teaching that described the whole human race as intrinsically corrupt. (This was developed from Augustine's teaching that we are a *massa damnata*, a damned mass). Salvation was said to consist of being covered with the merits of the blood of Jesus, while inside we remain a mass of corruption. For many Christians, until up to very recent times, such a self-identification blocked out any real sense of our true reality—that no matter what we do, we humans are fundamentally glorious, beloved children of God. Upon reflection, there can be no other conclusion than to say that Bruce's punitive and degrading soteriology implies an unscriptural demeaning of both God and humanity.

Christ's Teaching

Perhaps the very best critique of these ideas is found in the masterpiece we call the parable of the prodigal son. (Lk. 15:11ff) The father (God) is described as having absolutely no thoughts of punishment for his wayward son. He begins rejoicing from the moment he sees from afar that his son is returning home. All that is required of the son is that he return home. The father/God in no way stands on his dignity. Whole-hearted welcome and loving restoration (that is, salvation) is given *unconditionally*. The son is a sinner. He has strayed, become wayward, off the mark. When his suffering and the thought of his father's house bring him back on track, that is the end of the whole affair! There is no need for a guilt trip. No talk of offended dignity. No buying back the Father's good will. No need for expiation or for paying a penalty.

The son does denigrate himself and say, "I am no longer worthy to be called your son..." But the father absolutely ignores his son's shallow self-identification, *because it is simply not true!* He embraces and kisses his child, then says to the servants, "quickly bring out a robe—the best one—and put it on him; put a ring on his finger and sandals on his feet and get the fatted calf and kill it, and let us eat and celebrate." This robe doesn't cover corruption, but is a sign, together with the ring, that this person always has been and always will be the father's beloved child. The only thing enjoined on the sinner is to return and celebrate.

However, the negativity of our Christian consciousness has influenced even our reading of this marvelous parable. There is, of course, no title given to the story in the original text of Luke. But in our guilt-ridden perversity, we fixed on the offending, sinful son and for centuries have called it the parable of the prodigal son, whereas the obvious focus of the piece is on divine, unconditional, compassionate love.

In many other scriptural texts, Jesus strongly rejects this punitive notion of salvation. His teaching clearly supercedes that primitive way of seeing God as a very human-like person who follows the eye-for-an-eye-and-tooth-for-a-tooth concept of justice. This may have been a helpful system in early human societies, but Jesus proclaims powerfully that this is not the way God actually is. He forcefully tells us to abandon this law of retaliation and its theology. Recall Matthew ch. 5:38ff.: "You have heard that it was said 'An eye for an eye and a tooth for a tooth'? But I say to you, do not resist an evildoer... Love your enemies... Be perfect, therefore, as your heavenly Father is perfect." The parallel passage in the gospel of Luke (6:27ff) ends, "Be compassionate as your Father is compassionate."

The basic metaphor for God that Jesus consistently follows is that of a loving, non-fearful, non-punishing parent. The Abba (Aramaic for father) of Jesus does not look down at sinners and make conditions, saying, "You stop doing that, then I will love you; you do this, and I will receive you as my beloved child; you pay this penalty and make that expiation for your sins, then and only then will I cancel your debts and welcome you back." As John says, "God is love." Jesus insists that divine love is unconditional.

If you think about it, isn't it amazing and contradictory that to this day many Christian churches preach a Jesus-paid-the-penalty-for-our-sins theology of salvation one Sunday, while the next Sunday the message is God's unconditional love? Certainly the law of retaliation is part of our human baggage. Buddhism, too, insists on the law of Karma, which is also basically reactive. It has been entered into the universal human energy form field by centuries of such thought and behavior. We are constantly under its influence. But Christ's salvation is built on divine love, not retaliation. The very fostering of the attitudes and behavioral patterns of punitive soteriology is one major cause for the delay of that Second Coming of Christ which scriptural literalists so treasure.

All of this implies that the suffering and death of Jesus are not to be classified as identical with the primitive blood sacrifices of the Jewish religion. It is not the reality, but only the words and images from that culture and its rites that are used as metaphors to describe the great events of Calvary.

Another major question arises from the salvation model represented by the quotation from *Left Behind*. Bruce says, "…we are saved by grace through Christ, not of ourselves… he saves us."[4] The question, then, is how can another person save me? Is not my life and even my salvation my own responsibility? In the next chapter, we will lay the foundation for our response to this pressing question by presenting four helpful examples.

Chapter 21

SAVED BY CHRIST

Ask not
For whom the bell tolls;
It tolls for thee.

How can another person save me? Is not my life and salvation my own responsibility? Is our salvation a pure gift of God through Jesus? Do I really do nothing to gain salvation? All of these questions arise from an incomplete human self-identification. They betray our lack of enlightenment. If we had true consciousness, we would realize that the "other person" who saves us is not as "other" as we usually think.

We Christians should be embarrassed that we even formulate such questions. They point out the sad fact that an amazing amount of theologizing is done not with the Christ-Consciousness, but with a mentality of egocentric exclusivity, of devastating dualism. A great percentage of Christians still have little experience of the consciousness Jesus spoke from

157

when he said, "Love your neighbor as *your self.*" Paul had this Christ-mind, but labored to express it with a rather impetuous, inadequate vocabulary. Isn't it time that we develop modes of expression and a whole theology that is less open to desecration from unenlightened awareness?

The scriptural soteriology that we are presenting is built on the foundational reality that we humans are so truly one that what one person does belongs to all. What's more, if that one person's (e.g., Jesus') action is pure and powerful enough, it can enter into and transform the life of all. These ideas are not unfamiliar to most people and they have already been basically presented here, but it is time to flesh them out with some stories. The first was told to me by Sister Agnes Lee. It can be a test of your Christ-consciousness.

A Buddhist Monk

It seems that a certain Buddhist monk was attending a criminal trial. The accused person had unquestionably committed a terrible crime, was properly judged guilty, and was sentenced to an appropriate punishment. At the conclusion of the proceedings, just as the criminal was being led away, the monk went up to the person, bowed profoundly, and said, "Thank you. Thank you for taking my punishment for me." If this story is somewhat puzzling to you, think of it as a zen koan, let it work inside yourself, and then read on.

John Donne

Recall the well-known, but ever-to-be-repeated meditation of John Donne. In the winter of 1623, Rev. John Donne, dean of St. Paul's Cathedral in London, was lying in bed ill, when he heard a bell tolling for a person who had just died. The following lines are from his long meditation at that time.

> The church is Catholic, universal, so are all her actions; all
> that she does belongs to all. When she baptizes a child, that
> action concerns me… No man is an island, entire unto

itself; every man is a piece of the continent, a part of the
main [land]. If a clod be washed away by the sea, Europe is
the less, as well a promontory were... Any man's death
diminishes me because I am involved in mankind, and
therefore never send to know for whom the bell tolls, it tolls
for thee.[1]

Donne knew nothing of terms like holon and holographic, but
when he proclaims "it tolls for thee," we know that he has put on the archetypal mind of Christ. He knows reality as it is and experiences the glorious,
though sometimes painful, oneness of our be-ing.

The Hundredth Monkey

In the story of "the hundredth monkey,"[2] we have another striking
demonstration of the basic fact that all that is done by any individual within an energy form field belongs to all who share that field. The biologist Lyle
Watson relates how a group of Japanese scientists were studying a sub-
species of monkeys that live on some islands off the coast of Kyushu, the
southernmost of the four largest islands of Japan. There was also a colony
of the same primates on Kyushu itself. To attract them, the researchers
would dump sweet potatoes on the beaches for the monkeys to eat.

The little animals enjoyed the sweet new food, but, of course, they
had to put up with the sand and grit of the beach that stuck to it. One day
a young female, whom the scientists came to name Imo (potato), discovered
that by washing her potato in the sea it became free of grit and tasted better because of the salt. Imo showed this to her mother and others in her little group.

Well, monkey see, monkey do. More and more of the members of
the colony on Imo's island began to wash their sweet potatoes in the
water. Finally, at a certain number, a critical mass was reached. (Watson
arbitrarily put this at the hundredth monkey). That very same day, all the
monkeys on the other islands and on the mainland also began to wash
their potatoes!

When little Imo washed her sweet potatoes in the sea, she unconsciously placed this new behavioral pattern into the energy form field of her sub-species. It was an exciting, pleasant pattern. This began a kind of chain reaction in which the power of the new behavioral pattern grew and grew until it ended in the evolution of the whole group up to a somewhat better life. Imo was hardly aware of the social effect of her action. She did it for herself. Nevertheless, because of the holographic unity of monkey reality, the whole body of monkeys was changed. When we move to the human level, a higher degree of awareness can enter in and change all to love.

The Clock

The following metaphor can help us to better understand the actual process of salvation. Visualize a multitude of small pendulum clocks all fixed to a vast wall made of wood. Although they are all fundamentally the same kind of clock, each is engrossed in just doing its own individual thing, showing its own time and running independently.

Now suppose that one more clock is attached to the exact center of the wall. This clock is exactly the same as the others except that its "own thing" is to keep time exactly as it is meant to. It is following the plan and doing the will of the clockmaker perfectly. It is set right according to the flow of time, and thus shows true time. Finally the battery of this central clock is new, so its movement is powerful and true.

Because the wall is a sounding board, the rhythm of each clock spreads out to the whole wall in the same way as do waves in a pond. Each instrument influences all the others, but all is chaos and disharmony. Into this sad state of the clock world, come the powerful sound waves of the central clock. These beats are so strong and so true to the actual makeup of all the clocks that those near the center begin to attune themselves to the archetype. They rejoice in this entrainment of their movement because they realize that they are following their true self. The result is *shalom*—movement according to one's true self.

Gradually, the circle of synchronized clocks widens until a critical mass is reached. Suddenly the whole wall resounds to the rhythm of truth.

All the clocks, including the one at the center, while remaining individual, become one in the archetypal (Christ) clock that is impeccably expressed in the central one.

If we think of the placement of the true and archetypal clock on the wall as the first coming of Christ to our wall world, the second coming will be when the whole wall becomes one archetype dynamically attuned to one flow of energy. (More on the Second Coming of Christ later).

This metaphorical example limps along because the actual process of human salvation (whole-ing) is by no means so mechanical. Human beings are amazingly adept at devising behavioral patterns contrary to their archetypal nature. These blind, egocentric patterns also go into the human energy form field. They lodge in the field, which we all share, with such power that in spite of all the great men and women down the centuries who have actualized the Christ-Self, the critical mass has not been reached. Full human salvation (wholeness) is, as yet, a beautiful dream, an ideal which we must work for with our whole life energy.

Those early disciples who first experienced the glorious, archetypal human, the risen Jesus, were so enthralled by this experience of evolutionary truth and power that they concluded that full human "righteousness" was sure to happen soon. That foundational Christian vision was so powerful and dynamic that for them the Second Coming had to be just over the horizon. Sad to say, it is still yet to come. They were, it's true, mistaken about the timing, but not about the full-life-giving power, truth, and love of the archetypal clock, Christ Jesus.

Chapter 22

JESUS AS SAVIOR

*Enlightenment
Is a flower that blooms on the path
of waywardness.*

I clearly remember one afternoon in 1935 in St. James dormitory at St. Joseph's Military Academy in Belmont, California where I spent the first two years of high school. Some of us had just listened to a radio broadcast of the then-famous Father Coughlin from his devotional shrine near Detroit. (Later, sad to say, he became infamous for his anti-Semitism.) Talking with two or three classmates, I expressed my feelings and ideas about salvation. "All I want is to just get into heaven. I don't care about how high a place it is. Just as long as I don't go to the eternal flames of hell and manage to squeeze through the door of heaven, I will be satisfied." Although these were not my precise words, they do exactly represent my sentiments at that time.

Looking back now, I can't help but feel sad and even embarrassed by the incredibly low state of my Christ awareness at that time. Granted, I was just beginning the struggle to develop an adult ego, but those words still clearly show a lack of any sense of the glorious social dimension of salvation. It is also an unfortunate commentary on the consciousness of the general Christian community in those days that the church had not been able to instill in me any understanding of the evolutionary nature of the salvation process as rebirth into a wonderful new life. All I seem to have understood is: Avoid hell and get to heaven. I now know that this is frighteningly far from the vision that launched Christianity into human history.

So, building on all that we have presented in the previous chapters, we can now offer a more complete picture of human salvation as experienced by Christ Jesus and his disciples. We will base it primarily on the New Testament, but transpose it, when necessary, into terms more consonant with the many advances in human consciousness and knowledge made over the past twenty centuries.

Salvation certainly means far more than just avoiding eternal punishment and getting into heaven. It is more than receiving forgiveness for our sins. It is definitely not a matter of literally appeasing an angry God and meriting rewards for our good deeds.

Salvation has three major elements:

(1) We are *saved from* the powerful influence of unnatural behavioral patterns.

(2) We are *saved by* putting on those patterns of thinking, willing and acting that follow our nature as children of God.

(3) By following the creative pattern of evolution, we die to the limitations of life on this planet and are thus enabled to *rise to* a glorious new state of life in a new heaven and a new earth. Salvation is, by its very nature, evolutionary.

Following the law of creation (increase), we are made to be born into one state of life, to die to that state, and to rise to a higher life in which we actualize the whole (God) even more perfectly. Jesus Christ is savior because he placed this pattern into our universal human energy form field in a dynamic way, and by that very fact draws all humanity to new life.

The Aikido Principle

Jesus of Nazareth was a true and fulfilled human be-ing. He was impelled by his human nature and by the very nature of the creative process to manifest, to the full, life on this planet and then go through death to a new and greater manifestation of the infinite Source. One of the most amazing features of his evolutionary progress was that he used the energy of obstacles to accomplish his ascension to rebirth.

A good example of what I am trying to say can be drawn from Aikido. This mindfulness discipline is rightly called the path (*do*) of joining with (*ai*) energy (*ki*). Suppose that a person comes to attack you with power and force. Instead of resisting the attack, you go with the force coming at you. You take it to yourself, join it with your own energy movement, and use it for your own advantage. You are able to do this because your mindfulness is more perfect than your opponent's. "Where attention goes, energy flows." When two states of attention are in conflict, the energy goes with the more perfect one.

In such a process, you have changed opposition into cooperation, waywardness into righteousness, and, in a very real sense, evil into good. This is what I call The Aikido Principle of evolutionary progress. Jesus followed this principle all during his life, but especially in his passion, death, and resurrection.

Recall again his first baptism. After the great experience at the Jordan River, Jesus was "led by the Spirit," (the great creative drive) into the desert. This was necessary for integration. He needed time for the powerful new awareness of himself as child of God to work its way into all the elements of his psyche. As the power of his enlightenment spread into every facet of his life, his every thought, word, and action—every act of his senses, imagination, and emotions—came to be "born of God."

But even here, the aikido principle is seen at work. This process of integration was greatly helped and hastened by his being tempted to act against his nature as child of God. Satan (the ancient Hebrew word for enemy) tried to move him off the Path, but Jesus used the energy flow of Satan contained in his words of temptation to hasten his own definitive entry into the reign of God. Jesus' intention and attention to the divine will was stronger than the waywardness of the Tempter. However, at the end of his account of this testing time, Luke mysteriously remarks, "When the devil had finished every test, he departed from him until an opportune time." (Lk. 4:13). This next time came at the second and fully-definitive baptism of Jesus—his suffering, death, and resurrection.

Jesus And Evil

In his discourse the night before he died, John has Jesus say, "I will no longer talk much with you, for the ruler of this world is coming." (Jn. 14:30) "This world," for John, means the world of weak, fallen humanity that has a huge build-up of false behavioral patterns in its human energy form field. Its ruler is Satan, the personification of this misuse of the creative power.

Throughout history, the free will given to humans has been abused. We have thought, said, and done things contrary to the Creative Flow. These countless acts of waywardness, off-the-mark acts or sins, are all holographically present in the universal human form field. Taken together, they form a potentially immense influence on human be-ings. The Hebrews loved to personify. They called this concentration of wayward power the Enemy, the Devil, the ruler of this world, the Prince of Darkness.

Jesus experienced the pull of this Power just as we do, but with far greater awareness and sensitivity "For we do not have a high priest who is unable to sympathize with our weaknesses, but we have one who in every respect has been tested as we are, yet without sin."(Heb. 4:15)

When Jesus entered the garden of Gethsemane to pray on that night before his death, his profound enlightenment revealed to him that all the past, present, and future actions of humanity belonged to himself. This is what the holographic vision of true enlightenment teaches one. Impelled by his oneness with all humans, he deliberately fixed his attention on all the devastating cruelty, violence, greed, intolerance, hatred, pettiness, and ego-centricity—in a word, on all the sin of humanity. This attention activated that immense negative energy and Jesus accepted it as his own. To describe this movement of Jesus' spirit, the early Christians used the image of the suffering servant of Yahweh:

> Surely he has borne our infirmities and carried our dis-eases... he was wounded for our transgressions, crushed by our iniquities... by his bruises we are healed. All we like sheep have gone astray: we have all turned to our own way, and the Lord has laid on him the iniquity of us all. (Isaiah 53:4a 5,6.)

So intimately did Jesus take to himself the whole human burden of sin that Paul says simply, "For our sake he [God] made him [Jesus] to be sin who knew no sin, so that in him we might become the righteousness of God." (2 Cor. 5:21) To "become sin" was incredible suffering for the sensitive psyche of Jesus. Luke describes this agony, "In his anguish he prayed more earnestly, and his sweat became like great drops of blood falling down on the ground." (Lk. 22:44)

When we read the Scriptures, the critical point is the *story*, the inner teaching, not historical accuracy. So we can say that Genesis teaches us that it was in a garden that the first collective figure of humanity, Adam, felt the seduction of waywardness and fell. Then in the Jerusalem garden, a Second Adam, Jesus, employed the Aikido principle to perfection. Having taken in the power of evil, he used that power in following the creative Flow. This led him through death to life. All this is expressed in the letter to the Hebrews with extraordinary clarity. We quote the words again:

> In the days of his flesh, Jesus offered up prayers and suppli-cations with loud cries and tears, to the one who was able to save him from death, and he was heard because of his reverent submission. Although he was a Son, he learned

obedience through what he suffered; and having been made
perfect, he became the source of eternal salvation for all
who obey him... (Heb. 5:7–9)

Pure Love Transforms All

So perfect, pure, and impeccable is the spirit of Jesus after his ago-
nizing trial that when Judas came to the garden and betrayed him with a kiss,
that intimate sign of love itself, Jesus responded from the depth of his heart
and called his traitor "friend." In his appalling waywardness, Judas was doing
a necessary work. "At once Judas came up to Jesus and said, 'Greetings,
Rabbi!' and kissed him. Jesus said to him, 'Friend, do what you are here to
do.'" (Mt. 26:49–50) The devastatingly negative energy of Judas and all those
responsible for the crucifixion became Jesus' way to new life and glory.

"Enlightenment is a flower that blooms on the path of wa019-
ness." This sentence, which I discovered once on the bulletin board of a
temple near our school in Hiroshima, expresses in Buddhist terms the reality that in this life, sin energy itself is integral to the process of salvation. As
Paul says, "We know that *all things* work together for good for those who
love God." (Rom. 8:28)

His Return to the Formless Source

Empowered by his intimate contact with sin, Jesus was enabled by
the creative drive to make a perfect passage through self-dissolution to total
transformation. It is this behavioral pattern which he dynamically placed
into our human energy form field. When we, following our very nature,
entrust ourselves to this drive, we, too, are emptied so that we may express
the Whole more fully. We are saved. We are "Wholed." Jesus' physical death
was by no means the whole of the salvation process. His bodily dying was
the necessary external manifestation of a total loss of self called "The Great
Death." To actually attune one's self to the Formless, to the Infinite, our
self-identity must dissolve, until we temporarily end in no self.

The Great Death

In the scriptural account of his death, it is not difficult to trace Jesus' path to total detachment and loss of concrete identity. The quality and quantity of our physical possessions can have great influence in determining our actual self-identity. Jesus was stripped of all his possessions, even down to the garment he wore. (Mt. 26:56) He was identified as a Rabbi, a teacher, but "All the disciples deserted him and fled." (Mt. 26–56) Without disciples he, in a sense, lost status as a teacher. Then, too, his arrest by the temple authorities and rejection by the Jewish Sanhedrin in effect robbed him of his place and identity in Hebrew society; he is no longer a Jew. Treated by the Romans as a thing to be snuffed out, he loses his very dignity as a human being. As to his family identity, he gives this up, saying to his mother, "This [John, not I] is your son." And to John he says, "This is your mother [not mine]." Finally, in Psalm 22, he expresses his loss of every image of and "relationship" with God: "My God, my God, why have you forsaken me?" (Mk. 15:34)

Regardless of whether you fully accept these interpretations of the external events of Calvary, it is clear that Jesus died not just physically but preeminently psychologically. He has to "go to the Father." (Jn. 13:1) This meant attunement to the Formless. In the hymn praising the self-effacement of Jesus given in the letter to the Philippians, it is said, "he emptied himself." This emptying (kenosis) reached its climax in his return to the Source via the great death.

Christian tradition has always marveled at the love of Christ manifested on Calvary. Paul describes Jesus as one "who loved me and gave himself up for me." (Gal. 2:20b) To love is to discover oneness and to fully accept it. From the time of his great enlightenment at the Jordan, Jesus loved his neighbors—that is, all humans—as his own self. He accepted this identity so fully that he took to himself all our weakness and waywardness. It was enlightened love that transformed evil into good, death into life, suffering into glory.

Chapter 23

RESURRECTION FIRE

The candle is lit,
Revealing our goal in life -
Resurrection fire.

The Easter Vigil

I deally, it is Saturday midnight. The whole inside of the church has been bare since the end of the service Good Friday afternoon. The statues and pictures are covered and there's not a flower to be seen. It is totally dark inside; not even a sanctuary lamp burns. Outside the door a fire has been struck and blessed. From it the great paschal candle is lit. Now, holding the candle high, the presider strides dramatically into the darkness of the church, proclaiming as he goes, Lumen Christi—The Light of Christ! Once inside he pauses and those close by light their own candles from the Christ candle. He sings out "The Light of Christ" three times as he proceeds up the aisle. Each time more people light their candles, until every person is sharing the Light of Christ. Then all break into the triumphant song, "Glory to God in the Highest…"

I have participated in this grand Easter Vigil ceremony well over seventy times. I've learned about the symbolism of the midnight hour (the Source), the bare church (the loss of all on Calvary), the darkness (of death and Sheol), and, of course, the candles representing Christ. The first thirty times or so the vigil was all in Latin and began about six o'clock Saturday morning! Even now, it usually begins and ends well before midnight. Nevertheless, in spite of such modifications, it is a truly impressive service and the inner meaning does remain. However, I honestly wonder how much of that glorious significance I have ever been able to truly grasp. Have I even once gone out of this Easter celebration all excited, enthusiastic, eager to tell everyone, "Christ is Risen!"? The simple proclamation "The Light of Christ" actually epitomizes the gospel, but has it ever been incredibly "good news" for me? For most Christians? Has Easter ever really meant much more than new clothes, a family get-together, a special dinner, and an Easter egg hunt for the children?

As the Easter celebrations have followed one after another down the years, my sense of their inner reality has grown. But I sincerely feel that only within the last few years have I begun to actually appreciate the Paschal Event for what it is—a world-shattering movement to which I can willingly and joyfully entrust my whole life and death. I feel as if I have finally joined Peter, John, Andrew and Philip in becoming a Christian. To best present the light I have been receiving regarding the Resurrection, it will be useful to consider another vigil service. It differs from Easter, but nonetheless has profound meaning. I have only attended it two or three times.

The Bodhi Vigil

It is very early in the morning of the eighth day of the twelfth month. The dimly lit Sanun Zendo is full of silent figures seated in zazen. The energy in the room is intense. For some sitters this is the end of seven full days of sesshin. Others have only come the evening before to join in the all-night meditation vigil. We are near the end of the rohatsu sesshin. The ones I attended were from December first to the morning of December eighth. Other zendos hold the rohatsu whenever it occurs according to the lunar calendar, usually in late January. No matter, it is a cold time of the year. The all-night sitting is in commemoration of a very momentous event of two-and-a-half millennia ago.

Buddhism Is Born

It is again early morning of the eighth day of the twelfth month, now around 530 B.C.E. Siddhartha Gautama, later to be known as Shakyamuni Buddha (the sage of the Shakya clan, the Awakened One) is seated under a species of fig tree deep in meditation. For six years he has been a homeless seeker engaged in severe ascetic practices. Now, at the age of thirty-five he has turned solely to meditation. It is seven times seven days since he began this protracted period of sitting. Throughout this long night the temptations of Mara, the personification of the passions that overwhelm humans, have brought Siddhartha to an intense state. (Again we see the importance of negative stimuli—the aikido principle.) Finally, as he looked up at the morning star that early dawn, he broke through to complete and definitive enlightenment. It was truly the dawning of the Day. He discovered with radiant and blissful clarity the true nature of reality. This light shattered all illusions and drew him into the Flow of Life so powerfully that he realized that for him there was now no need for rebirth into this world. Buddhism was born under the Bodhi Tree (the pipal fig tree). Its whole purpose is to assist any and all to this same awakening and transformation.

The "when" and the "where" of the foundational Buddhist experience are clear enough, but the "what" and the "how" of it need further reflection, both for their own immense intrinsic value and because they can form the background for a deep understanding of the Christian resurrection event. What happened was that Siddhartha broke through to the intuition of Be-ing and was transformed. To appreciate what this Western philosophical expression really means, we can break it down into Be-ing, intuition, and transformation.

Intuition of Be-ing

The Be-ing that Gautama discovered was Be-ing Itself, both uncategorical and universal. It was manifest to him in the morning star, the fig tree, and his own be-ing. What he became aware of, though, was not just human, plant, or mineral be-ing, but Be-ing pure and simple. Unlimited Be-ing is manifest as any and all be-ings. This brings us to the *how* of his experience, to intuition. To actually perceive unlimited Be-ing, he had to go beyond his ordinary way of seeing reality.

The mode of perception that we humans use to experience reality is usually both pluralistic and dualistic. What Gautama entered into was a mode of perception that can be called unity consciousness or pure Be-ing awareness. To better understand this we need to start with the principle that *every be-ing is conscious*. Every kind and level of the event we call be-ing has its own built-in awareness. "Conscious" means to know (scious) with (con). Consider the most fundamental event of all, the Movement of the Source into Form. This Be-ing event is an intelligent, conscious, action of a responsible Subject—the Divine Person. Every be-ing event manifests and shares in the consciousness of the Creator Be-ing according to its make-up. The myriad of unique and separate be-ings have a mode of perception (a consciousness) suited to separateness. This is our ordinary pluralistic knowing. We are forever categorizing and splitting up things. When we turn this kind of awareness to ourselves, we separate ourselves from everything else in the universe and from Be-ing Itself! We can even look at ourselves as objects. This basic subject-object mode of perception can be called dualistic.

There is nothing wrong with pluralistic or dualistic perception. It fits its own aspect of reality. However, if this is all we use, we end up in illusion, because all the innumerable separate be-ings and all subjects and objects, while being diverse, are at the same time one. As the early Greek philosophers discovered, reality is not just many, it is also truly one. This one is not an ordinary number one that begins a series. This oneness is boundless, beyond all categories, and it, too, has a built-in awareness. Under the Bodhi Tree this boundless awareness took over Gautama's psyche and he was transformed. He saw not just the star, the tree, and his own self, but within all he discovered infinite Be-ing and became radiant with bliss. It is this knowledge that Buddhists call *prajna*, transcendent wisdom. In the title of the constantly recited Heart Sutra prajna is called *prajna paramita*—perfect wisdom, that which has reached the Other Shore. We can say that the other shore is the unity side of the one-and-many nature of reality.

Transformation

We become what we experience. We are transformed into what we really know. When our stance toward reality is only dualistic and pluralistic, our lives are a succession of many events with only partial, if any, integration. Some people do go beyond egocentrism and integrate their lives around family, company or nation, but all such dominant objects of our perception and will are restrictive. Ultimately, none of these restricted integrating centers can satisfy us, because our hearts are unlimited. A person like Gautama, who is totally infused with the intuition of boundless Be-ing, enters into fully holistic integration. This is the total transformation we are speaking of here. Of course, it is not something imposed from the outside. Nor is it a gift from God, as from the Great Other. Rather, it is the actualization of the true Self. It is Be-ing OurSelf.

A Universal Person

The integration Siddhartha experienced unites him with all be-ings without exception. He discovered that his very nature, as a manifestation of Be-ing, is that of a universal person. His Self-identification includes everyone and everything. There is only one Self, which we all are! This state of Self-awareness is brought out in the Buddhist legend that says that even as a newborn infant, he declared: "in the whole universe I alone exist!". Until a practitioner can repeat these words out of personal experience, that person is not yet a complete Buddhist. A true person is Universal/individual.

Light

All movement is in wave form. This is true because all the movements of be-ings are only concrete manifestations of the absolutely fundamental movement of the Bipolar Ultimate. Be-ing Itself is the movement of the Formless Source into Form; then Form returns to the Source, which moves into higher Form, and so on. This is the basic vibratory movement of reality. In Genesis (1:3) the primal creative statement is, "Let there be Light." This is "first day" light, not the light of the sun, moon, and stars which, in the creation myth, did not appear until the fourth day.

When a person allows the primal movement with its consciousness to arise into awareness, that person, we say, is en-*light*-ened. This was the radiance Siddhartha's companions saw in him. After that December morning experience Gautama continued meditating. His friends saw his blissful state and asked him to teach them. At first he remained silent. Integration takes time. Finally, moved with the compassion that arises out of prajna, he broke his silence and gave his famous first instruction in the Deer Park of Benares. This great Self-actualized hero continued teaching for over forty years.

The Christian Experience

The circumstances and characteristics of the foundational Buddhist experience are clear and basically accessible. What of Christianity? To begin with, when and where did Jesus enter into that experience out of which Christianity was born? Was it on the bank of the River Jordan at the time of his first baptism? That might well seem to be the time and place. However, important as that event might have been, both scripture and tradition have always given the dying and rising of Jesus as the foundational event. We call it the Paschal Mystery. Of the two elements in the Paschal Event, the dying is clearly for the sake of the rising. It is the resurrection to new life, the rebirth to a higher manifestation of Be-ing that is *the* Christ experience.

Paul asserts the primacy of the resurrection throughout his writings. In one of his earliest letters, we find him stating in no uncertain terms:

> ...if Christ has not been raised, then our proclamation has
> been in vain and your faith [entrustment] has been in vain
> .... But in fact Christ has been raised from the dead, the first
> fruits, then at his coming those who belong to Christ. (1
> Cor. 15:13–14; 20; 23)

Isn't it remarkable that the experience of Jesus upon which all Christianity is built is a post-death event! As a holy person of prayer and compassion, Jesus undoubtedly had many deep spiritual experiences during his restricted life on our planet, but it is his rebirth into a whole new level of life after his passage through death that is special to him. It follows that the whole of Christianity is (or should be) geared to assisting us to share through the same death the same rebirth to a life of glory.

As is obvious, there are special practical problems arising from the fact that the foundational Christian experience happened after the founder's death. First of all, how on earth is it to be communicated? The Buddha could and did teach for many years after his enlightenment. Obviously, the communication of Jesus was quite different. How was he to teach after his death? Again Paul, in the same early letter, is very clear:

> For I handed on to you as of first importance what I in turn
> had received: that Christ died for our sins in accordance
> with the scriptures, and that he was buried, and that he was
> raised on the third day in accordance with the scriptures,
> and that he appeared to Cephas [Peter], then to the twelve.
> Then he appeared to more than five hundred brothers and
> sisters at one time, most of whom are still alive, though
> some have died. Then he appeared to James, then to all the

> apostles. Last of all, as to one untimely born, he appeared to me. (1 Cor. 15:3–8)

Jesus was no longer visible to our ordinary perception, so he needed witnesses who would experience his total transformation and then proclaim this good news. Besides that of Paul, we have Luke's concise account of this experiential transmission and the commission it included.

> After his suffering Jesus presented himself alive to them [the apostles] by many convincing proofs, appearing to them during forty days and speaking about the kingdom of God.... [He said] you will receive power when the Holy Spirit has come upon you; and you will be my witnesses in Jerusalem, in all Judea and Samaria, and to the ends of the earth. (Acts 1:3, 8)

Since living witnesses of the after-death transformation of Jesus were absolutely essential to the foundation of Christianity, it follows that we must acknowledge that the Christian Path is not founded only on Jesus' own experience. In a unique way, it is also based on Jesus' transformation as experienced and transmitted by the first disciples. What, then, did they transmit to us?

He Is Alive Again!

When Peter and the others met Jesus after his death, their first and overwhelming impression was that he was alive again. To appreciate what this meant to them, we have to forget our present-day assumptions about immortal life and put on the Jewish attitudes toward death that prevailed at the time. After death people went to Sheol, the Underworld. In Jewish cosmology this was an area literally underneath our surface world. Above were the heavens, and above all this God ruled from on high. Sheol was a place far from God, a dark non-world. It was dark because the creative vibrations were of so low frequency there. In Sheol, existence itself was very shadowy and the people were mere shades. The deceased were so dead that they were incapable of real activity. They couldn't even praise or thank God. (Isaiah 38:18) Sheol was conceived of as a kind of power which drew all through its gates, called in our English translations, "the gates of Hell." (Mt. 16:18)

For centuries, the Hebrews pretty much thought that Sheol was the end of the human life line. Once entered, there was no return to active life. That is one reason why it was so important to live on in one's children. However, there gradually arose in the Jewish writings a strain of hope that death and Sheol were not terminal. Finally, in the second century B.C.E., clear traces of belief in a return to life are found. By the time of Jesus there seemed to be a great debate going on about resurrection from Sheol. The strictly observant Pharisees affirmed the possibility of a return to active life, while the Sadducees, the influential priestly aristocracy, denied such a thing.

About thirty-five years after the death of Jesus, when speaking to the Jewish council (Sanhedrin), Paul declared: "'I am on trial concerning the hope of the resurrection of the dead.' When he said this, a dissension began between the Pharisees and the Sadducees and the assembly was divided...Then a great clamor arose." (Acts 23:6–7,9a)

Given such a confused state of belief, it is understandable that the first thing Jesus had to do after his death was to prove that he was still alive, and powerfully alive. "He presented himself alive to them by many convincing proofs." (Acts 1:3) We can also now appreciate the force of the words the disciples used to express this phenomenon "He is risen!" They were saying that after death he went to the Underworld, but that he has now physically "risen" from down under, even up to God's heaven above. Not only that, he promised to actively be "with them all days" until they, too, could rise up to heaven in new life. "I will come again and will take you to myself, so that where I am, there you may be also." (Jn. 14:3) Christians today are so used to words such as these that they have come to have little effect on us, but given the consciousness of the first Jewish disciples, the simple fact of Jesus' resurrection was incredibly "Good News."

What Kind of Life?

That Jesus was actually alive after death was a marvelous discovery, but the even more crucial question for us is what kind of life the disciples saw manifested in him. Historically, we don't know for sure about the details of those pristine encounters with the Risen Jesus, but the details are not all that important. We have enough revealing evidence both in the written testimony of the early church and in the immense change in the lives of the disciples. What is certain is that what the disciples saw in the Risen Jesus was *radical Be-ing* expressed purely and freely. Christianity was born out of the intuition of Be-ing just as Buddhism was. Jesus' post-death experience was the beatific, transforming vision of full and perfect Be-ing.

In Luke's gospel the dying words of Jesus are, "Father, into your hands I commend my spirit." His life force (spirit) is unreservedly open to the Creative Source. John describes Jesus' passing on as "going to the Father." (Jn 13:1ff) Through his "great death," Jesus entered into the after life perfectly attuned to the creative action of the all mighty Source. The loss of his bodily life was the way through which he became totally empty. (Note that this does not mean annihilated. He simply had nothing exclusively his own.)

This very emptiness attuned him to and brought him to the "Father" who is empty of all actualized forms but full of all potential forms. The essential nature of the Father is to actuate these forms, to give Be-ing. Because Jesus has died to his former life, like a seed falling into the ground, the Source can raise him up to a new and incomparably higher level of manifested Be-ing. Jesus rises as the glory of God.

Light

Recall what we said about Gautama being transformed into light because of his intuition of Be-ing. If this can happen even while a person is in this flesh, imagine what the be-ing of Jesus became upon his post-death rebirth. Again, I would maintain that it is because of the radiance that Paul and the other witnesses saw in Jesus, that John has Jesus describe himself as light, "I am the light of the world. Whoever follows me will never walk in darkness but will have the light of life." (8:12) It was this personal light which drew Paul onto the Damascus Road. This great and pure Light-Movement of the Triune Reality is now entered into our universal human energy field. If we follow the Light-Jesus by our entrustment, we will truly walk in "the light of life."

Oneness - Love - Joy

In the intuition of Be-ing/be-ing which is the foundation of his risen life, Jesus discovered the existential oneness of all reality. As we have noted many times, at the constituative level reality is bipolar. There is a Formless Pole and a Form Pole. Only when these two are in Movement do you have Being or Existence, and their Movement is an alternating current. The Formless moves into Form; the Form returns to the Formless Source. These three, Source, Universal Form and Alternating Flow, although a trinity, constitute *one* Existing Be-ing. All reality is this one Be-ing, existent in many manifestations.

Jesus, knowing himself to be such a manifestation, has to say, "The Father and I are one." (Jn. 10:30) By the same token, he must say to any and every be-ing, "The Father and you are one. You and I are also one. We are all one Be-ing manifesting. Though many, we are one. Besides our own individual selves, we are all one Self." This is the Self Jesus refers to when he says, "When I am lifted up [on Calvary and in resurrection), I will draw all to my Self." (Jn. 12:32) In this text, he could just as well said, "to Our Self". This same one-Self-consciousness is expressed in the great commandment, "Love your neighbor as your Self."

To discover oneness is to enter into love. As we all know, love is a state of oneness in which diversity is not lost. Real love, like reality itself, is bipolar oneness. If the outcome of oneness is love, the fruit of love is joy. Joy is the radiant bliss that arises out of love. Christ Jesus is drawing us all to pure joy. John has Jesus speak to the Abba Source the night before his death, "But now I am coming to you. I speak these things in the world so that they [the disciples) may share my joy completely." (cf. Jn 17:13) True consciousness always brings profound joy. The risen Christ is continually drawing us to full awareness and perfect joy. This, too, is Good News indeed.

Resurrection is Evolution

There is no question that Jesus and his disciples, through their intuition of Be-ing/be-ing, discovered the evolutionary nature of all reality. The whole universe is by its very nature called to constant growth, to ever-greater levels of be-ing manifestation of Be-ing. An immense Movement of the divine Spirit has been released into our human form field by Jesus' resurrection. It can lift up you and me and the whole universe to be born of the Spirit into a life of eternal abundance. This, I must say, is the most exciting part of the Good News. It, above all, can electrify our lives with Resurrection Fire.

Chapter 24

COMMITTED TO
CHRIST ENERGY.

The Way says,
"Lose your self in ME
And you will find your Self."

I n 1975, I was asked to go to Germany and direct a ten-day retreat for a group of Japanese Sisters working in Cologne. On my return visit, I was able to visit Lourdes, Munich, Jerusalem, Katmandu, and Bangkok. Lourdes was one of the great highlights of that trip and of my life pilgrimage. I didn't go there for any particular healing; rather, I just wanted to immerse myself in the special energy of the place, in the vital force many Christians call "Mary." Although it was past the peak of the season, there were still many pilgrims and their faith in Mary was deeply moving. I have never been to a holier shrine. My plan to make an all-night zazen vigil in front of the grotto had to end at about two a.m. because of the rain, but the profound effect of my visit was in no way frustrated. It was a pilgrimage of deep devotion.

Although many Protestant communities have no place for Mary in their Christian devotion, and in some cases are firmly opposed to her, nevertheless there remains an immensely powerful attraction and devotion to Mary in the Christian (and even Muslim) world, especially among Anglicans and Episcopalians, Catholics, and Orthodox. To understand more clearly who the Jesus is that Christians have entrusted their lives to, it should prove helpful to consider our devotion to Mary of Nazareth.

Marian devotion is a striking example of our need for idealization and archetypalization. We humans are forever looking for heroes and heroines, for ideals and archetypal figures. We instinctively need a person who can embody the highest form of some creative energy. By devotion to such a person, we connect with that special energy and are transformed.

So powerful and necessary is this process that we can take almost anyone and build the person up to the ideal, the archetypal status. For better or for worse, look what humans did to Hitler and Mao Tse Tung. There is no doubt that John F. Kennedy and Jackie Kennedy were charismatic people, but our drive to idealize them elevated their time in the White House to the level of the mythic Camelot.

Idealizing can occur even in the face of actual historical data that show the person to be far from ideal. It is easy to understand how we can not only create a mythic figure but even go one step further and supply pseudo-historical data, so the figure becomes a powerful embodiment of the energy we desire to actualize in ourselves.

The Divine Mother

Every enlightened understanding of reality, every true spiritual path, arises out of the intuition of Be-ing/be-ing. One great insight into life, which goes back far into pre-historic times, is the sense that there is a motherly, caring, even loving, life-giving power at work everywhere. From the earliest times this visceral intuition has been expressed in feminine imagery about the source of everything.

The visceral need to connect with this life-giving energy became personified and symbolized in the "Divine Mother." Museums are replete with ancient statuettes of this Mother. Black Madonnas, which well antedate Christianity, are still reverenced in Europe. In some cultures, the Divine Mother eventually evolves into the great goddess, who would sometimes be so cruel as to demand blood—even human—sacrifice. Nevertheless, the feminine imagery of the Source as caring, gentle and life-giving is forever fixed deep in the universal human energy form field. To this day, it is constantly being brought up into consciousness, especially in times of trial and trouble. Christians have found and, to some extent, created Mary of Nazareth to be just such an archetypal Divine Mother.

Guan Yin

Before taking up the question of Mary, consider for a moment the immensely powerful and popular figure Kuan Yin (sometimes written Guan Yin). This is the Chinese name for Avalokiteshivara, the bodhisattva of divine compassion. In the original Sanskrit, this figure is masculine. Kuan Yin (in Japanese, Kannon) is feminine and very motherly. Tibet has both the masculine Chenrezi and the feminine Tara. There is absolutely no certain evidence for or against the actual historical human existence of a unique individual Kuan Yin. However, because the whole focus is on the archetype, historical details about the ideal person are not important. In fact, true historical accuracy is not even essential. Pseudo-historical, mythic details can do us quite well, thank you.

Just as with Kuan Yin in Mahayana Buddhism, so in Christian piety it was an easy step to attach the ancient Divine Mother devotion to Mary and to make the mother of Jesus into our Universal Mother. It was nothing unusual that when the persecuted Japanese Christians of the early seventh century wanted to hide their devotion to Mary, they connected it with devotion to Kannon and created images of "Maria Kannon." I can take you to gardens in Kyoto where such images are still preserved and even treasured.

Mary of Nazareth

There is, of course, a great difference between Kuan Yin and Mary because Mary unquestionably lived among us as an historical person; she was the mother of Jesus. There is also no reason to doubt that she lived in Nazareth. But there is little, if anything, more that we can present as certain history about the mother of Jesus. The two great sources of details about Mary are the first two chapters of Matthew and Luke, respectively. But modern scripture scholarship has liberated us from taking these sometimes contradictory chapters as accurate historical accounts of Jesus' infancy and Mary's part in it. The purpose of these chapters is theological teaching, not historical reporting. We will discuss the point at greater length when dealing with Jesus and the historicity of all four gospels.

Here, suffice it to quote the highly regarded Catholic scholar Raymond E. Brown, "It is best, then, to settle for the observation that there is no way to know exactly how historical the infancy Narratives are, or to know where Matthew and Luke got them." [1]

As to the rest of the New Testament, very little is given about Mary. Paul never speaks about her, except to state that Jesus was "born of a woman." (Gal. 4:4) The Acts of the Apostles mentions her once, as being with the Apostles after Jesus' resurrection. John brings "the mother of Jesus" into his gospel at Cana and at Calvary without even giving her name. Apart from the infancy narratives, the synoptic gospels mention Mary only five times—enough to name and establish her as Jesus' mother. No wonder John L. McKenzie concludes his section on Mary in his *Dictionary of the Bible* speaking of "...our almost total lack of genuine information concerning the life and person of Mary. [2]

So again we ask, where did devotion to Mary come from? The fact that she was the mother of the savior Jesus certainly is one important element. On the other hand, I would maintain that the powerful, ancient drive to approach the divine as feminine is even more fundamental to the devotion. In a way, it was better not to have a lot of historical facts to deal with. Without them, it has been easier to idealize and archetypalize her, so that Mary of Nazareth, the mother of Jesus, has become the Divine Mother of the whole human race.

The Christ Jesus of Faith

What are we to say about the Christ Jesus whom the disciples met after his death? In the resurrection appearances, they encountered a person to whom they could give over their lives completely and who transformed them because of their total entrustment. Filled with the power and joy of this evolutionary encounter, they went out bearing witness to this person and encouraged all peoples to the same transforming entrustment (faith). We are called to this same process today. But again, who is the Jesus in whom people are to put their faith?

The extraordinary Letter to the Hebrews delineates the Christian Path beautifully: "'let us run the race set before us, fixing our eyes on Jesus, the founder and finisher of our faith." (Heb. 12:1–2, my translation) Which Jesus is focused on here? Again, we must answer that it is not primarily the historical Jesus, a male Jew of our first century, but rather an archetypal person who actualizes in his resurrection the evolutionary destiny both of every human being and even of the whole cosmos. The focus of the archetype is on Bar Nasha (Son of Man) and on the Logos (Word).

The Glory of the Lord

The Christ Jesus that Paul focuses is always an archetypal person. One typical text is 2 Cor. 3:18: "So we all, with unveiled faces, are mirroring the glory of the Lord and are being transformed into the same from glory to glory, as by the Lord, Spirit." (I've used my own version in order to translate the verb *Katoptrizomenoi*, which literally means "mirroring.") As mirrors, we humans are not cold and hard but living and pliable. We are transformed into what we face. This means that if the Jesus we encounter and reflect is primarily the historical Jesus, then the Christian Path would be calling us all to be transformed into first-century Jews! But Paul is clear that we are to mirror the *glory* of the Lord and be "transformed into the same from glory to glory." Paul consistently uses Lord to refer to Jesus. Both scripture and tradition clearly teach that the glory of Jesus is what happened to him after his death, not that of the Jesus of ordinary history.

We must always keep in mind that Christianity is a spiritual path arising out of the resurrection experience as it happened to Jesus and as it was witnessed by the first disciples. It is now presented to one and all for its actualization in us. *Everything in Christianity is at the service of the resurrection process.* This is to be said not just of the writings of Paul, but of all the Christian scriptures. Paul uses his own experiences and those of his converts to convey the resurrection message. The gospels, too, are focused on the risen Christ. Their primary purpose is not to report the history of Jesus but the mystery of his archetypal being as revealed in his post-death resurrection.

Of course, Jesus of Nazareth does have a factual history. The evangelists do use facts. However, the people of the first century in no way had the passion for historical accuracy that we are so caught up in today. It's worth reflecting that they did not have any of the accurate instruments of reporting we are used to, such as printed books, newspapers, radio, T.V., and the Internet. Many people were illiterate. Communication was verbal, built on memory. What was important to communicate was not historically accurate data but the inner, dynamic meaning of a person's life—those universal, archetypal, and ideal elements that concern us all and can transform us.

Reflect for a moment on how you read the writings of the New Testament, especially the gospels. Do you read with the desire to know whether what you are reading is historically true? If you find out that some part of the gospel is fiction, does this diminish the value of that section for you? Isn't it true that most of us are governed by a powerful tendency to read this way? However, three points must be made about this demand of modern readers. First, even in the case of the gospels, we can never arrive at factual certainty except in regard to the broad outlines of Jesus' life. Second, unless we give up the demand for detailed historicity, we will never be able to attune to the gospels as they were written. And third, if we *do* give up this attitude, the vital power and dynamism of the sacred writings can work within us today.

The Gospel Text

The only text of any gospel that can truly be called accurate is the original manuscript itself or its exact copy. But in the strict sense, such a text is not available to us. We certainly do not have any original manuscripts, and the copies we have all have differences. The earliest gospel fragment that we have at present is a tiny part of John's gospel dated by most at the very least one hundred years after the death of Jesus. The earliest copies we have of complete gospels come from the third century, around two hundred years after the first gospel (Mark) was probably written. What is more, all the manuscripts are handwritten and no two are exactly alike. However, scholars have done a fine job in providing us with an adequate Greek text. But then comes the notoriously difficult and inherently inaccurate process of translation into modern languages. Textually then, true historical accuracy, aside from broad outlines, is unattainable to us.

How to Read

Happily, though, detailed historical accuracy is not really important. Without it, in fact even because of its lack, we are quite able to contact the Lord of glory whom the sacred writers are presenting to us. When we give up all those modern demands, we will be free to read the gospels as they were written. Certainly, with the texts we have today, illumined by centuries of tradition, we can be flooded by the true gospel message. The New Testament does truly put us in contact with the living Christ of the resurrection. The life-giving Spirit works not through accurate historical data, but through the ideal and archetypal Christ who is assuredly presented in the sacred text, such as it is.

Focus again for a moment on the first-person pronouns used by Jesus throughout the gospel text. It would be ridiculous to assume that every time Jesus says I, me, my, or mine, he is being accurately reported, as if his works had been tape recorded and then written down. These pronouns obviously are intended to express the all-inclusive self-identification of Jesus, the universal person, not the all-exclusive self-awareness of Jesus as an individual. Taken this way, we can each find our self in the Christ of the New Testament. If we take "Jesus" as the name of the historical male Jew of Nazareth and "Christ" to indicate the archetypal human ideal, it becomes quite fitting that the followers of the gospel path are called not Jesusians, but Christians.

To properly focus on Jesus as our ideal universal person has many crucially important fruits. First, this focus on the archetype is the foundation for reading the scriptures. With it, not only can we read them as they were written, but this is also the only way that their transforming powers can be released into our lives. Second, it is only this universal Christ that we can see both in ourselves and in all people. This is the only Christ in whom we are all one.

The poem of the zen master Hakuin in praise of zazen was regularly recited in the Sanun Zendo. The last two phrases were my favorites: *Tosho, sunawachi Renge Koku. Kono mi, sunawachi Hotoke nari.* "This very place is the Lotus Land. This body person is Buddha." I would often read these lines to myself as, "This very place is the Kingdom of Heaven. This body person is Christ." This reading was quite valid, because both Christ and Buddha refer to the same universal being. This is the self spoken of in the great commandment, "Love your neighbor as your *self.*"

Third, it is this Christ through whom all people are saved. "No one comes to the Father [this is salvation] except through me" can only refer to Jesus as a universal person who is the actualization of what it means to be a true human being.

Finally, the term Christ has come to indicate not just the universal human (Bar Nasha) but also the Logos, the totally universal pattern of all creation. This Christ is "The image of the invisible God, the first born of all creation." (Col. 1:15). As John says, all things come into being through the Logos (Word). All beings, without exception, share this form. In this fundamental sense, the book you are holding, the rose in your garden, the car you drive, everything is Christ.

Although the poet Joseph Mary Plunkett uses masculine pronouns for the Logos Christ, who is beyond gender, nevertheless his poem is touchingly true.

I see his blood upon the rose
And in the stars the glory of His eyes,
His body gleams amid eternal snows
His tears fall from the skies.

I see His face in every flower
The thunder and the surging of the birds
Are but His voice - and carven by His power
Rocks are His written words.[3]

Using a focus on Christ in nature as our example, we turn now to consider more about how we are to actually connect with the Christ who transforms us.

Chapter 25

FINDING CHRIST
IN NATURE

Lakes, mountains,
Brooks, flowers and trees
Never sin.

Mindfulness is the fundamental discipline of every true spiritual path. Since it is the quality of one's mindfulness that is crucial, it doesn't matter all that much what objects one chooses to be attentive to. Nevertheless, among many possible choices, nature does hold a special place, so this chapter will deal with how to find God/Christ in the remarkable universe in which we humans live.

When we choose to be deeply aware of people, we will certainly find Christ in them. But people are wayward, full of non-Christ tendencies and actions. People can hurt us. When we focus on ourselves, we find that we are also mixed up. The Logos-Christ manifestation within each of us is clouded. Nature, on the other hand, is impeccable. A morning glory never sins; it is quite literally a pure manifestation of the glory of the "Morning Star," Christ (2 Peter 1:19). To use the language of Paul (2 Cor.3:18), "the glory of the Lord is there for us to mirror by our mindfulness."

The Hindu poet and mystic Rabindranath Tagore was standing on his verandah one morning looking at the scene before him. The sun was just rising through the trees. As he continued to gaze, a veil seemed to fall from his eyes. He saw the whole world bathed in a wonderful radiance. With this light of beauty came waves of joy and bliss. It was experiences like this that gave depth and universal appeal to his great poetry. If we learn to gaze at nature in mirror mindfulness, some degree of this experience is accessible to each one of us.

Shinmin

The modern Japanese poet Shinmin Sakamura sings beautifully about nature, especially flowers.

A Flower blooms purely	Saku mo mushin
falls purely	Chiru mo mushin
and without complaint	Hana wa nagekazu
lives the now	Ima wo ikiru

In my translation, I have rendered mushin as "purely." This describes a heart (shin) that has within it no (mu) opposition to the creative life force. In other words, a flower is sinless, impeccable. Even if a seed falls into a crack in the blacktop of a parking lot, the flower doesn't complain (nagekazu). It simply manifests its being in its given circumstances. Nor does it envy the flower two meters away that is growing in fertile ground. And Shinmin notes that a flower doesn't live *in* the present, it *lives the now*.

A flower actually contains all the mystery our hearts long to behold. Another of Shinmin's poems expresses the richness and mystery of flower life.

What is best?	Nani ga ichiban ii?
A flower is best.	Hana wa ichiban ii.
What is so good about a flower?	Hana wa doko ga ii ka
What is best is that a flower	Shinjite saku no gii
blooms with entrustment.	

(Author's translation)

The key word here is *shinjite,* trusting. A flower's life is entrustment, total surrender to the creative Flow of the Source. Isn't it remarkable that flower can be read flow-er?

We become what we mirror in ourselves through attention. When we allow into ourselves the impeccable life energy of flowers, rocks, and animals, we are drawn from our waywardness into the path of pure life. This pattern of living purely in the Flow of the Source is what we call Logos/Christ. Jesus of Nazareth, as the embodied Logos, says, "...I do nothing on my own, but I speak these things as the Father has instructed me." (Jn. 8:28). Nature lives the Pattern, the Christ, beautifully.

Mindfulness

I learned about mindfulness experientially one crisp winter day in the hills of Kamakura across the road from our language School. I was walking by myself on a trail along one side of a small valley. The other side was a typical winter scene—a slope covered with bare trees and thickets, with a few pines and other evergreens interspersed here and there. I *stopped*, stood still, and stared at the scene.

At first glance it was nice, but not all that arrestingly beautiful. However, as I *kept looking* I became aware of an immense variety of shapes and colors. The vegetation was brown, russet, tan, gray, green and even chalky white, in amazingly subtle pastels. As I gazed, the shape of each tree, bush and outcropping of rock came to stand out as *individual and unique*. Fascinated, I kept gazing. Next, the distinct clarity of details began to merge into a remarkable *harmony*. No shade or shape was out of place. Everything was melding into one "sweet especial rural scene.". (G.M. Hopkins)[1]

Here, sad to say, my ordinary mind interrupted the process. It effectively stopped the movement into *communion*. I began to reflect about the scene and about my gazing. Even at the time, I knew that if I could have continued to gaze without adding on mental reflections and labels, if I had not begun thinking about how I could share this with others, I would have lost myself in the harmonious oneness of the Self. The subtle, quiet, nothing-unusual reality there before my eyes was radiating the Whole. In philosophical terms, all the trees, shrubs, and grasses of that hillside were holons containing and impeccably manifesting the Whole. Through mindfulness, my perception was becoming attuned not just to the many but even to the One. If my simple, bare attention had not wavered, I could have entered in and discovered the Self.

When we quiet the pluralistic and dualistic mind, the rest of the process is almost inevitable. The heart will take its natural course to God. A new mode of perception will arise in the psyche. In the light of non-dual consciousness, we will experience the coincidence of the many and the one. This is true contemplation.

Incidentally, it is this contemplative ideal which has effectively kept me in the Society of Jesus these many years. Our Founder, Ignatius of Loyola, gave us as our primary mode of living the finding of God in all things. A true Jesuit is said to be a *contemplativus in actione*, a person who is contemplative in his activities, no matter what. What I didn't really understand for many years was the crucial importance of mindfulness practice to realizing this ideal. It was only after I had been a Jesuit for about thirty years and had begun the disciplined attention of zen that I experienced that contemplative seeing in the Kamakura hills.

Contemplative Awareness

Contemplation is a matter of direct awareness. It is a mode of perception in which you share in the very being of, say, *this* daffodil. Every movement, every act of existence, has a built-in self-awareness. We call this *consciousness* (con = cum = together with; scious = scire = to know, be aware). This daffodil's being is constituted by both its act of existence and its built-in self-awareness. If, through simple, bare attention, you come to forget your own self-awareness (your ego), you can actually share in the self-awareness of this daffodil. Your identity melds into the identity of the flower. In this sense you become the flower.

Such a contemplative communion can only happen when you go out of your preoccupation with the self-centered awareness of your being as separate. *Subject-object perception must drop away.* Once in this contemplative mode of perception, it is an easy step to move into the Self-awareness of Being Itself. Plants, because of their purity, are excellent for such contemplative insight. We end in becoming one with Being Itself and therefore with all beings without exception. This is why zen teachers say that the universe is in every grain of rice, and why Ignatius of Loyola calls on us to find God in all things.

The How-To of Contemplative Awareness

Consider the words I italicized in the account of my experience on the Kamakura hillside.

Stopped. The first step on the contemplative path is to stop. Often this means to stop physically. You are walking in thick woods. Suddenly a beautiful meadow opens out before you. To enjoy the scene, you stop walking; this for the sake of simplicity of attention. While walking, you have to keep one eye open for rocks, roots, puddles on the trail. So to put your full attention on the meadow, you stop. Meditation, zazen for example, is the same. You stop all physical movement so as to enter into mindfulness. Even the walking done during meditation time is done in simplicity on a clear, level place as you fix your total attention either on each step or on the same focus you've been using while sitting.

However, interior stopping is vastly more important and, sad to say, immensely more difficult. In order to reduce and then stop our ordinary pluralistic/dualistic awareness, we draw our attention away from the past and the future, from abstractions and reflections, from expectations and worries, from all such distractions, and move into simple, bare attention to one focal point (e.g., breathing). This can even shift into attention without any object.

Kept looking. If we were perfectly disciplined in attention, one moment of bare attention would bring us into unity consciousness. As it is, we usually have to keep on looking and looking, often plagued by distractions. This is the hard part and takes real effort. We need to persevere until non-dual consciousness begins to arise in our psyche. When this happens, the effort to focus turns into effortless effort.

Individual and unique. Take again mindfulness to this flower. Our path to true awareness begins in the individual existence of this particular flower. The eternal One is to be found in this here-and-now flower. This flower holon, precisely as unique, is what leads us to experience the Common Whole.

Harmony. Put yourself again beside a lovely meadow you have discovered in a forest. Having stopped, you keep looking at all the unique details. As you continue to give bare attention to the meadow, the beautiful harmony of all the various elements of the scene arises in your awareness. Each flower, each blade of grass, fallen log, tiny shrub, and bit of moss—all separate—come together. Each unique, they join in a commonality. Their diversity is existentially compatible with their being one. This is the bipolar universe before your very eyes. Think of how colors in nature never clash. The tints and shades we humans put together are often in disharmony. Isn't it because, except when humans interfere, nature is always in the Flow, which means not just harmony but oneness.

Communion. Harmony is only a passage to communion. Not only are all the elements of the meadow scene together in one energy Flow, *you* are in that same Flow, too. As you keep gazing, you enter into the oneness of the meadow and all things. In this experience, the duality of subject (you looking) and object (flowers, grass, etc.) drops away. You enter into what truly must be termed "Divine Awareness." You and the scene, while existing as many beings, are at the same time One Being. Just as each being has its concomitant singular and unique awareness, so Being has Unity Consciousness. Mindfulness brings us all the way to the One Ultimate Awareness we all share. In the state of full consciousness we must say to each tree, rock, or blade of grass, "We are one Self. You are Me. I am You." This Being/being Self-Awareness is full enlighten-ment...the goal of mindfulness.

Risen Awareness

To come to even more clarity about the progress and fruits of mind-fulness, imagine that you are out hiking and, having just come around a bend in the trail, you stop to gaze at the grand scene of a lake surrounded by mountain peaks. A couple of minutes later a hiker comes by and asks, "What are you doing?" You answer, "I'm looking at the beautiful scene." Ten minutes later, another hiker finds you fascinated with the lake and the peaks and asks the same question. This time you answer, "Look at the mar-velous colors and shapes. They're all so unique, but so together!" (Note that already there is no "I" in your statement.) Some time later, a hiker who has seen you from afar asks somewhat impatiently, "Do you realize how long you have been standing there blocking the path?" You answer, "Oh. I really don't know. A few minutes? No time at all." (Actually, you've been there for almost 30 minutes, but time and space have begun to collapse into the-ever present universal. Archetypal consciousness is taking over in your psyche.) Finally someone asks, "What on earth are you doing?" This time all you can do is tremulously murmur, "Lake! Mountains! Brook! Trees!" Not under-standing, the person looks at you with a puzzled frown. But the hiker is not where you are. The two of you are in different modes of perception, in dif-ferent worlds. No longer just a subject looking at objects, you are within the coincidence of opposites found in the lake and the peaks and trees and your-self. All are in the Reality of One Source, One Flow, One Universal Pattern. You have entered into Eternal/temporal, Formless/form, One/many *life*. Mindfulness has brought you to into the intuition of Being/being, into the new life of ongoing Resurrection.

Chapter 26

FINDING THE ARCHETYPE IN PEOPLE

"More is in you."
On the church wall and housegate;
"I am with you."

There is a remarkable dialogue about God between two black women in Alice Walker's novel *The Color Purple*. Shug, the older woman, asks Celie, "Tell me what your God look like, Celie." Embarrassed, Celie finally admits, "He big and old and tall and grey bearded and white. He wear white robes and go barefooted."[2] Their dialogue continues until Shug, "looking like a big rose," tells of her own experience of God.

> She say, My first step from the old white man was trees.
> Then air. Then birds. Then other people. But one day when

I was sitting quiet and feeling like a motherless child, which
I was, it come to me: that feeling of being part of everything, not separate at all. I knew that if I cut a tree, my arm
would bleed. And I laughed and I cried and I run all around
the house. I knew just what it was. In fact, when it happen,
you can't miss it.[2]

Note the progression of Shug's movement into enlightenment. She
went from nature—trees, air, birds—to other people. Finally she discovers
that nature, people, and herself are all one. Having dwelt on finding Christ
(God in Form) in nature, we turn now to other people and to self.

It is certainly true that nature is a special area for Christ discovery,
but no focus of enlightenment is more important than human beings—self
and others. The Christ teacher, Jesus, could hardly have accented this focus
more. His special commandment is that we love one another. We find little
about nature mysticism in the New Testament, but the crucial importance
of human relationships and oneness is stressed throughout. To love is to
discover oneness and fully accept it. To love humans is to discover that we
are all one Self and to live according to this reality, no matter what people
we contact.

So fundamental is this human oneness to the Christ Teacher that he
placed it as the basic norm to use in judging whether we are with him or not.
"By this everyone will know that you are my disciples, if you have love for one
another." (Jn. 13:35) The self-identity out of which the statement "my disciples" arose is that of the human archetype. To say "you are my disciples" does
not mean that the followers are living like a first-century male Jew. Rather, it
says that we are living according to our dynamic, all-powerful human archetype. Reflect for a moment on how you are aware of yourself and others. Are
you consistently conscious of what glorious beings we all are?

What Are We?

One year in the early nineties, Sister Agnes Lee and I spent almost
a month in Belgium; she giving a series of lectures, the two of us directing

retreats. One morning a friend took us to the beautiful old city of Brugge in West Flanders. While visiting a large church of Our Lady near the heart of the city, I noticed a balcony built high up into the side wall of the sanctuary. Our friend explained that this balcony was immediately connected to a house built right beside the church, the house of a wealthy, influential family of the fourteenth and fifteenth centuries, the Grunthuse. Having this special place made it easy for the family to attend Mass. Interesting as the balcony was, even more impressive were the words written on it, *Plus est en vous* (More is in you). This was the motto of the Grunthuse, as we found out when visiting their grand house. There over the main gate was the motto again, not only in French but also in Flemish (*Meer is in u*).

When we ask "What am I?" or "What are we?", the full answer is breathtaking. There most certainly is far more in you and me than we are usually aware of or even dream of. True, each of us is a unique, individual, very limited subject, but at the same time we are the embodiment of the human archetype (Bar Nasha) and of the Universal Pattern (Logos). We are Christ. We are not bundles of energy only at age three; all our lives we are nothing but divine energy, the Trinity individualized. At root, each human person is a radiant being, an evolutionary dynamo reaching for resurrection.

Just as the spiritual path is built on and for the intuition of Being, so the path of human relationship arises out of and leads towards the intuition of *human* being. This intuition must, of course, be experiential, but it should be useful to see how our intellects can help us to genuine experience of our humanity.

We Are Evolutionary Beings

The question "What is a human?" is huge. Up until modern times, traditional Western ideas about humanity pretty much followed the Greeks and Romans. In their paradigm; we are split into body and soul. The body is mortal; the soul is immortal, never dying. Human nature is a fixed set of qualities and powers, according to which we move into action and live our lives. Each person is born with this nature but we can and do act contrary to its best advantage. Every human is created as an image and likeness of God.

When we turn to Buddhist teaching, we find quite a different anthropology. The Heart Sutra, echoing very ancient teachings, speaks of humans as being made of five *skandhas*. The root meaning of skandha is a heap, an aggregate. Here it refers to five elements which heap up together to form a human being. The five elements are form (material form), sensation, perception, mental formations, and consciousness. These five elements are always changing in relation to themselves and to all other beings, in a process that has been going on since time immemorial and will continue on and on.

What we think of as one individual subject is simply the heaping together of the five skandhas. Since human be-ing is nothing more than this changing process, Buddhists hold that there is no independent, fixed self-identity. It is an illusion to think that "I" as a human being have a permanent essence.

The brief treatment I've given here of both Western and Eastern anthropology is most inadequate, but at least we can see that the West has traditionally accented the fixed nature, an essence, as the foundation of human be-ing, while the East stresses process, the fluidity of no fixed essence. I feel that we can learn from and profitably combine both analyses.

The picture of humanity that I believe is emerging in our time is a model which accepts both process and stable form. (The same paradigm is emerging for God and for all created reality.) Note the word stable. This differs both from the eternally fixed idea (essence) of Plato and the pure process of Buddhism. On the one hand, each of us *is* an individual form field. You and I are each the one great energy Flow of the Power Source individuated in this particular subject.

Our forms have stability. When you go to sleep at night, you do so in your special form. When you get up the next morning, you continue living according to your same basic form. On the other hand, there have been changes in both your body and psyche during the night. We are always the process of evolution. The Christ Jesus who died on Calvary had his own individual form. When he rose from the dead, this form underwent a huge evolutionary change into a new and glorious human life. Whether you analyze humanity into body and soul or into five skandhas, the important point is, I feel, that all human beings are evolving.

Both as individuals and as a species we are *stable beings in process*. This process is simply the movement of the creative drive of the Power Source to manifest life more and more abundantly. Jesus of Nazareth, both as Christ and Logos—that is, as archetype of humanity and of all creation—declared out of his all-inclusive Self-awareness that he came that we might have life and have it more abundantly (Jn. 10:10). It is eminently true that *plus est en vous, meer is in u.* More is in you—more life, new and greater life, resurrection. This is our potential. If we all give our attention to this, we will all be speedily transformed. We need to look at ourselves and others as resurrection-bound beings. Each time we see a human person, we are seeing the whole potential of the Spirit individualized, no matter what condition the person is in.

Just as in beholding Nature, so in our human relationships everything depends on where we fix our attention. If we only see the dark blemish on one of the rose's petals, we will never join the rose in its impeccable life Flow. If we constantly judge people, looking at their defects, we cannot possibly discover our oneness with them. Such attention may lead to some sense of oneness in our weakness and misery, but this will never bring us to joyful union.

If people always remain other to us, love will escape us. If we consistently fear people as hurtful, how can we celebrate communion? We are taught to say, "There but for the grace of God go I." What true vision sees, in even the repulsive, is Christ and it leads us to say, "There am I!"

The Real Self

During our month in Belgium, Sister Agnes Lee and I directed a number of retreats. Our general theme was our Christ-Self. At one monastery the retreatants, almost all lay people, were such a small group that our presentations could sometimes become a kind of dialogue with them. One woman, after two days of hearing about and meditating on her true Self, couldn't stand it any longer. She objected strongly and said that all we had presented was fine, but she wanted to get down to her "real" self—the self that is weak, perverse, dark, and sinful. We told her, of course, that in no way do we deny these elements in our human makeup, but that we deliberately wanted to focus on the truly real self, the Christ Self, because where attention goes, energy flows. The self that will grow and be actualized in our lives is the one we are attentive to.

That woman, I would say, was exemplifying the fixation Western society has on our weakness and waywardness. This attitude is not true humility but a perverse work of the ego. Consider how approvingly we repeat Shakespeare's dictum, "To err is human, to forgive divine." Reflect how the suppositions here are all wrong. First of all, it is a highly dualistic saying. Its ordinary sense is that God is divine and we are in no way divine, that we are errant creatures. This dualism is itself a false assumption. By our very nature, we share in divinity. But it is even more misleading, perhaps, that we accept error and sin as the distinguishing characteristics of humanity! If this is our usual mind-set about ourselves, how can we ever come to experience that glorious human archetype, Christ, who is the very foundation of the existence of each of us?

To keep on beating our breasts and declaring ourselves to be weak and sinful is not full and true realism but a terribly incomplete vision that leads to illusion and defeatism. I sincerely believe that this false view is more pervasive and perverse than we might be aware of. Reflect for a moment on how you habitually perceive yourself. For example, if you are a Presbyterian, has the Calvinistic teaching about the pervasive corruption of your human nature ever disturbed you? Do you accept it and live by it? Or reject it? If you are a Lutheran, does Luther's insistence on your weaknesses—weakness so great that you are saved *sola gratia*, by grace alone—ever make you wonder about the value of your good works, whether your effort is of any value at all? If you are a Catholic, has it ever bothered you to say just before communion, the most precious moment of the Mass, "Lord, I am not worthy to receive you"? Have you ever really considered the kind of self-identity that is behind this traditional declaration? The phrase itself originates not from Jesus but from the words of a Roman centurion who asks

Jesus to heal his servant from afar, because "...I am not worthy to have you enter under my roof." (Lk. 7:6) Jesus, in turn, praises the man, not for his feelings of unworthiness, but for his faith. He sees him not as unworthy but as a person of that true vision and faith that releases the healing power of Christ.

Recall, too, that in the scripture texts where Jesus invites us to "Take and eat; take and drink," there is no mention at all about conditions, let alone feelings and declarations of unworthiness. Jesus saw every human as worthy of healing and new life, because he always saw through to the Christ potential in each one. His attention was on the Real Self, and because of this, Christ energy flowed in all his human relationships. This is the pattern for our lives today.

Speaking to people of all times and places, a Letter of John says:
By this do we know that we have passed from death into life,
if we have love one for another. (I John 3:14)

Chapter 27

BECOMING CHRIST IN THE MASS

*We are dying to break
Bread together at the banquet
Of the Risen Self.*

O n my mother's side, I belong to an old English family that kept to Catholicism all during the centuries of persecution. There is a family story about the time that a priest came secretly to the family estate, Hopwas House, shortly after the birth of a baby there. After a young lad had been sent up a tree to watch for redcoats (the government soldiers), the harried priest asked the lady of the house, "What will it be, Mistress Haskew, a baptism or a mass?" Mistress Haskew responded, "Please God, we shall have both." Then, as the story goes, they did.

This deep appreciation of the Mass is also evident in a letter which came into my hands after the death of my eldest sister, Pauline, two years ago. Before my mother died, she wrote a farewell letter to Pauline. The language is a little Victorian, but the faith is radiant. She begins, "Dearest Pauline, To you, my eldest child, I am going to bequeath the most precious thing I have ever possessed with all that goes with it: my love for the Holy Mass." It is safe to say that these two examples echo the feelings of Catholics everywhere. Certainly, from the earliest days, the Lord's Supper has been at the heart of Christianity.

It was toward the end of my years of teaching at Hiroshima Gakuin that I read "The Constitution on the Sacred Liturgy," one of the first documents promulgated by the Second Vatican Council of the Catholic Church. I read it in my room seated Japanese style on a floor mat. I'll never forget how moved I was. Here was a Roman document in fairly readable language that spoke directly to my heart. Tears actually ran down my cheeks.

In paragraph ten it called the liturgy, especially the Mass, "the summit toward which the activity of the Church is directed, at the same time it is the fountain from which all her power flows."[1] In a later document, the Mass is called the source and summit of the whole Christian life. (Lumen Gentium, No.11)[2] For the early Christians, the "breaking of bread" and drinking the ritual cup of wine was such an important place for encountering Christ that they called it The Lord's Supper. This, it seems, was not because Jesus had instituted the rite, but because when they performed the rite in community, they encountered the real presence of the Lord. It was a mystical experience for them. This chapter will conclude our investigation into where and how we experience the Christ and become transformed.

Energy Accessing Rites

The Mass is a highly sophisticated ritual with roots in very ancient, so-called primitive rites of initiation. From time immemorial, humans have entered into the energy fields of both nature and the past through rituals. Take a tribal dance performed before a hunt. By vividly acting out a buffalo's characteristic movements, the stalking of the hunters, and the final killing, the people all enter into the world of hunting and buffalo energy.

The vivid dance accesses the future buffalo hunt because it is a means of gathering and fixing the attention of the whole tribe. To make their attention even more powerful is added *intention*. Attention takes the people into the bison energy field and intention directs the flow of the energy toward the death of the animal. After a dynamically performed hunting dance, the next day's hunt is simply the working out of what has already taken place at the attention/intention level of reality. If attention and intention are maintained without weakening, the result is inevitable. The same forces are at work in dances and rituals to heal sickness. In this case, the power of attention/intention is directed toward producing a healthy person. Voodoo is sometimes used the other way, to create illness.

The other great use of ritual is to bring the energies of the past into the present, especially in rites of initiation. Some tribes native to Australia are models of this type of ritual. Their culture is based on and follows the Primordial Time when their Divine Ancestors established their way of life. The archetypal events of this mythic Beginning Time are reenacted by the use of sacred place, symbols, chants, and dramatizations. The neophyte is immersed (baptized) into the energies of the Past time and thus takes on the tribal way of life. He or she dies to the childish, incomplete life lived so far, enters into a new form field, and rises to the new and full life of the divinely originated culture.

So rituals can actually draw us into various energy fields, including those of historically past events. As an example of a ritual that makes the past operative in the present, consider the Jewish Passover.

The Passover

In Jesus' time, as in all previous generations, the Jewish people reenacted the Exodus from Egypt as one of the great defining events of their history. They still do today. The Passover celebration connects them with the events of Egypt, the Sinai, and the River Jordan. The whole Passage with all its energy is stored in the universal human energy form field, but in a special way in the form field which constitutes the real entity called Israel. By their memorial service, the past is made present and the creative power of the original Passover continues to draw Jewish people into their distinctive way of life. The ritual of the Lord's Supper, in its origins, was situated within the Passover celebration. It is the same ritual, but changed.

Christian Initiation

Traditionally, the rite of initiation into the Christian life is composed of two sacraments, Baptism and Eucharist. Toward the end of the first millennium, the special anointing which came toward the end of the baptismal ceremony was gradually celebrated on its own and became a separate sacrament called Confirmation. In recent times the original unity of Baptism and Confirmation is being somewhat restored. As to the events that these rites connect us to, the Christian churches have always been in agreement. The general introduction to *Rites of the Catholic Church* expresses the tradition succinctly: "Through the sacraments of Christian initiation men and women are freed from the power of darkness. *With Christ they die, are buried and rise again.*" (Italics added)[3]

This statement only echoes Paul's teaching. As to baptism he says: "We have been buried with him by baptism into death, so that, just as Christ was raised from the dead by the glory of the Father, so we too might walk in the newness of life." (Rom. 6:4) As to the energy we actualize in the Lord's Supper rite, Paul is just as dynamic: "For as often as you eat this bread and drink this cup, you proclaim the Lord's death until he comes." (1 Cor. 11:26) In his re-phrasing of the New Testament in his book *The Message*, Eugene Peterson renders this verse: "What you must solemnly realize is that every time you eat this bread and every time you drink this cup, you reenact in your words and actions the death of the Master. You will be drawn back to this meal again and again until the Master returns." [4]

Faith Memory

We have already insisted on attention and intention as integral to any effective ritual. As is obvious, for a rite of initiation we must add both memory recall and faith. It is recall that connects us with the past. But the power of these events will not touch us unless we have faith—that is, unless we are open to and entrust ourselves to receiving their energy. It is no accident that after presenting the bread and wine as dynamic signs of his passage through death to the eternal banquet Jesus prescribes, "Do this in *memory* of me." To this the liturgy immediately adds, "Let us proclaim the mystery of *faith*." (Italics added)

The Sacrament

The Mass is divided into the Liturgy of the Word and the Sacred Meal. The second part, the Lord's Supper, is described in three ways: as a sacrament, as sacrifice, and as containing the real presence of Jesus Christ. These three, of course, are intimately intertwined. We can consider them in order.

A sacrament, simply put, is a sacred sign. That it is a sign is of crucial importance. I believe I am echoing tradition when I say that there are four major sign elements in the ritual: 1) placing the bread and wine separately on the altar, 2) saying the words which also separate the two ("This is my body,…This is my blood"), 3) breaking the bread, and 4) consuming the bread and wine as a sacred meal. Separation of a person's body and blood means death, and this is clearly indicated by the separation of the sign elements both in words and in placement. The actual breaking of the bread further dramatizes the death memorial.

Jesus' death was a rite of passage to a new and exalted life in the Spirit. I would find the sign for this resurrection in something very simple and obvious, in the consuming of the bread and wine. These two, which signed death in their separation, now signify return to life by becoming united in the communicant. Having a sacred meal with all the other people present is the most important part of the resurrection sign. To eat together celebrates oneness. In ancient societies, one did not eat with enemies. One of the scriptural symbols for the unity of life in heaven is a sacred meal. The whole ritual of the Lord's *Supper* is a sign of the glory and unity of resurrection life.

Sacramental Access

At the risk of being redundant, we must face some fundamental questions again. Why did Jesus tell us to do all this in memory of him? How is it that a ritual like the Mass can actualize for us the power of those past events? Why does this rite of initiation plunge us into the very passage Jesus made through death to a new Path of Glory? Answers to these questions will prove this sacramental rite to be a brilliantly devised means of access to the power of the very events it signifies.

Recall again that everything any human person does is preserved holographically in our common and universal form field. Some actions stored there are weak. Some have strong influence. Our egocentric, negative, wayward activities do influence the rest of our race, but have the built-in weakness that they are contrary to the unlimited power of the Flow. Deliberate lack of attention can keep them weak. But in the case of impeccable actions which radiantly manifest the human archetype (the Christ), there is immense latent power.

The passion, death, and resurrection of Jesus were so pure and archetypal, so perfectly the movement of the Spirit, that they have stored into our form field all the power we humans need to actualize our divine potential. In the rite of the Mass, all the elements for effective access to this transforming power are given to us. The memory recall and the ritual signs focus our attention and intention on the actual events themselves. When we perform the ritual with faith, the power is released and we are plunged into the Christ passage to new life.

Sacrifice

One word traditionally used for the wafers of unleavened bread usually used at Mass is host, from the Latin *hostia*, meaning victim. That the Mass is a sacrifice is obvious from the fact that the rite connects us with Jesus' death and resurrection, which was clearly a sacrifice. This word comes from *sacrum facere*, to make holy. In a sacrifice you give up something in order to gain something better, something more holy. Jesus gave up his life on earth through his death and was raised to a wholly (holy) new level of life. By so doing, he put this process in all its purity into our common form field, into the soul of humanity. When we access it by faith memory, the same sacrificial process is actualized in our lives. Through the Mass ritual, we literally share in the great salvific sacrifice of Calvary.

Real Presence

I wonder if there is any Christian teaching that confuses people more than the doctrine of Jesus' real presence in the sacrament of bread and wine. We love the idea, but it is perplexing. Most confusion comes, I'd say, from people forgetting the sign character of the ritual. During my seminarian days at the Jesuit theologate at Alma, California, the "spiritual father" of the community (nowadays read "spiritual director") was giving a talk to all of us in our chapel. He told us that theologians had discovered that something like twenty-four miracles were needed for Jesus Christ to become really present in the sacramental bread and wine! I think that I swallowed this at the time, but now I must say that it is atrocious theology. Some Catholic theologians, though, still hold that Jesus is present in the physical bread and wine through the miracle of transubstantiation. I would suggest that this revered teaching is not only unnecessary but also misleading.

The idea of transubstantiation grew out of the medieval synthesis of Christian theology and Aristotelian physics. According to Aristotle there is a reality called the *substance* of bread. Remove the substance and you no longer have bread. Substance means stand (*stare*) under (*sub*). It stands under qualities of bread such as shape, weight, color, and taste. These are added to substance and are called accidents. These qualities can and do change, while the substance bread remains. Thomas Aquinas and others taught that at Mass, when the priest says, "This is my body" and "This is my blood," God removes the substances of bread and wine and puts in their place the substance of the Risen Christ Jesus. This is transubstantiation. The substance changes; the accidents all remain exactly the same.

Even if you still accept Aristotelian physics (though, as I understand it, most scientists do not), this neat explanation of the real presence is unnecessary. In fact the Church has always taught that the presence is neither metaphorical nor physical but sacramental. There is no need at all for intrinsic change in the bread and wine. The only change that does happen is that they are consecrated signs, whereas before the ritual words they were simply bread to be eaten and wine to be drunk. Now they have the added sacred function of being holy signs. It is through these ritual signs that we access the actual historical events of Calvary, which are always present in our human form field. By ritual reenactment the very physical dying and rising of Christ, Jesus is made vitally present to us. This is very real presence indeed.

To The Future

There is one huge difference between the initiation rites of the Australian natives, for instance, and those of the Christian path. The bush people recall the past so that their present society can model itself totally on Primordial Time. The rites, as I understand them, are highly conservative and are centered on the past. The Christian rites are progressive and evolutionary. It is true that by graphic and immensely meaningful signs both Baptism and the Mass do bring the past into our present, but at the same time they lead us into a new and evolved future. These rituals challenge us to actualize our divine potential. They offer the impetus to move all humanity into a dynamic age of cosmic renewal.

Chapter 28

ALWAYS A PILGRIM

Let us spiral upward
In the intimate, dynamic Pattern
Marana Tha!

We begin the final chapter of this book by taking you to the Rose Room at Mercy Center. This is fitting, because it is a special place where I and many meditators have made genuine advances on the consciousness pilgrimage. It is, let us say, the fourth day of a meditation intensive retreat. In the early morning about thirty-five of us are gathered in our quiet room. I will sit with everyone for the first thirty minutes before moving across the hall to the Aspen Room to begin individual consultations about meditation and related matters.

During forty-seven years of directing retreats I have talked individually with retreatants thousands of times. From this experience I know that, like each person before me in the Rose Room, anyone who seriously enters on the meditation path will come, at least now and then, to a state of perception that I sometimes characterize as "being home." This state is the immediate goal of our pilgrimage. One moves from being a subject looking, for example, at one's breathing as an object, to a much more direct state of *conscious being.*

A New Mode of Perception

Philosophically, this simpler mode of perception can be described as the self-awareness of being. Theologically it would be termed *divine self-consciousness.* Spiritually we call it *enlightenment.* However we describe it, the actual experience is a many-splendored thing. It can vary from a brief, momentary shift of awareness, hardly noticed, to a huge change of perception that lasts a lifetime, It can be a world-shattering, highly emotional upheaval or a rather cool, quiet intellectual insight with little more emotional content than a deep peace. Sometimes its concomitant sense of oneness is shallow and scarcely noticeable. Other times a person discovers all-embracing love—an exhilarating oneness with everyone and everything. According to individual character, one person will gracefully follow the path of gradual, incremental awakening or "commonplace kensho." This is the most usual path. Another person will crash the barriers to awareness with sudden, even dramatic breakthroughs.

No matter which path you find yourself on, two of the fundamental characteristics of true insight into Reality are bound to ultimately arise to your consciousness. For the moment we can call them *the intimacy* and *the dynamism of God.* These two have been my own experience, and I will end my tale with these two wonderfully heartening aspects of the divine quest.

The Intimacy of God

"God is more intimate to me than I am to myself." This astonished cry of St. Augustine has echoed in the hearts of Christian meditators for sixteen hundred years. Perhaps an even more accurate statement of our deepest Reality is that of St. Catherine of Genoa: "God is my being, my me…"

Catherine is speaking out of the effusion of her mystical experience, not out of philosophical thinking; however, we can legitimately look at her insight intellectually because all true philosophy and theology are rooted in mysticism. Her experience arises out of Reality which can be capsulated in three statements: (1) God is Being Itself, not *a* being; (2) Being Itself is Personal, and (3) Being is Self-aware. Consider these three in order.

God is Being, Not A Being.

Pause for a moment and reflect on this assertion. Does it not, perhaps, demand a profound shift in your conception of God? For me it represents the final unpacking of that insight of thirty-one years ago, "God is different." (See Chapter 14) If we conceive of God as "a being," this implies that the Divine is simply one among many who are in being, just as the expression "a rock" indicates one stone among the many that are in the state of rock being. In such a conception of God, it is valid to line up plant being, animal being, human being *and* divine being. However, to do so makes God other to all other forms of being, just as human is other to mineral, plant, and animal being. Some people go so far in this dualistic thinking as to call God "The Great Other." Even though you put God as the highest form of being, if you line up the Divine along with all the other forms of existence, you end up making that which is common to them all—being itself—more universal than God! All the myriad of beings in existence, including the divine, turn out to be one in being, not in God. In this scenario God is a being and so are we. We are one in a super-reality called being itself. Something is disastrously wrong here.

I remember struggling with these very questions as I walked the campus of St. John's University in Collegeville, MN, that autumn of 1966. My insight had long since shifted about God, but the dualistic patterns in my thinking persisted. It took years for my intellect to catch up to my intuition. Finally I was able to drop the concept of God as *a* being and rejoice in God as Being Itself, personal and all-pervasive. For years I have quoted St. Paul, "In God [In Being Itself] we live and move and have our being." (Acts 17:28) Can there be anything more intimate than this? God is the ultimate being of everything. Although it would be highly confusing, to say the least, to baldly state, "I am God," nevertheless your body right now, along with the book you are holding and the earth under your feet, are all Divine Being manifesting as you, book, and earth.

In the story related in Chapter 17, Joe E. Brown describes his experience: "I felt God's arms around me, in a way I cannot possibly describe." Struggling to express his enlightenment, he uses the image of an embrace. He certainly does not mean that God embraced him as another person would. In fact, he "cannot possibly describe" such intimacy. The comedian has shifted into the Self-awareness of Divine Being as present and manifesting in his very own existence.

Hildegarde of Bingen uses the same metaphor to express her experience: "God hugs you. You are encircled by the arms of the mystery of God." [1]. St. Mechtild recounts, "The day of my spiritual awakening was the day I saw—and knew I saw—all things in God and God in all things." And Meister Eckhart gives voice to Christian non-dualism when he says, "God created all things in such a way that they are not outside himself, as ignorant people falsely imagine. Rather, all creatures flow outward, but nonetheless remain within God."

Being is Personal

To speak of God as Being Itself may sound quite impersonal, but, as we have already discussed, Being is always personal. Return again to that fundamental experience of the Judeo-Christian tradition, the burning bush experience of Moses (Exodus 3:1ff). God's name is revealed as I AM. AM indicates that the Energy Flow we call God is not restricted to any particular kind. "AM" is simply the One Being manifest in all kinds of being. "I" indicates that Being is personal. Since a person is a conscious, responsible being, God must be said to be the doer responsible for the event we call being, however and wherever it happens. Everything that happens is a personal act of God! This is how intimate God is.

Being Is Self-Aware

Reality *at all levels of manifestation* has built-in self-awareness. There is consciousness, self-knowing, concomitant with every act of being. This is so because everything in existence is the manifestation of Being Itself, which is perfectly Self-conscious. Begin with a daffodil or your breathing or the simple act of counting. Quiet your mind by being totally attentive to the daffodil. Maintain this attention and you will subtly shift, first into the self-awareness of the flower and ultimately into the Divine Consciousness Itself. This is enlightenment.

This perception is not engaging in an *idea* about the Great Other or in an *image* of the loving Father up there. Rather, it is entry into the direct Self-awareness of the Divine Being, in whom we are all one I AM.

To forget oneself and enter the Divine Consciousness creates a major shift in the way we see reality. This is the *metanoia* (shift of awareness) that Christ Jesus urged on us all. One's life begins to be lived from a new point of view. Our viewpoint and our action point shift from subject-object perception and egocentric action to Divine Life. Thus it is that we enter the Reign of God.

The Dynamism Of God

Return with me one final time to the early morning Rose Room, as we begin a day of a meditation intensive retreat. The sound of the *mokugyo* (wooden drum) has called everyone to their cushions or chairs. The bell has rung and now, to unite and intensify our meditation energy, we begin chanting the ancient Celtic pilgrims hymn, "The Deers Cry" (More often called "Patrick's Breastplate"). In the course of this touching chant three times we sing out, "I arise today." More and more I realize the truth of this affirmation. This is what life is all about—today and every day, past and future. We are made to arise to ever higher and more glorious manifestation of divine life. Being Itself is creative and to create means to increase. All beings share in this intrinsic drive to evolve, to spiral out and up to more abundant life-manifestation. We are all pilgrims climbing the sacred mount of creation.

Without any planning on my part, it turned out that I began writing this final chapter on December 31, 1999—the last day of the year, of the century, and of the millennium. As the clock moved past midnight, the whole world joined in a sense of moving on to a new time. However, the truth of the matter is that the ever-creative movement, not only of the human race but also of all creation, is not just on to another flat segment of time, but to ever higher-levels of life itself. Despite many retrograde slips, the basic movement is evolutionary. This is what I mean by the dynamism of God, the Divine Source. The intrinsic drive of Being Itself is to manifest in ever-higher and more glorious forms of life.

The first Christians saw this character clearly in the very being of Jesus of Nazareth. Their experience of the risen Jesus was an intuition into Being. They saw his resurrection as an archetypal example of what all humanity is moving towards. They knew him as the pioneer of the Promised Land, the leader who can draw all humanity to new life and lift all creation to be "a new heaven and a new earth." (Rev. 21:1) "I [Jesus] have come that you may have life and have it more abundantly." (Jn. 10:10)

Jesus' first coming happened so that he himself could rise to new life and thus put this evolutionary pattern more firmly and powerfully into the universal human energy form field. His second coming will take place when a critical mass of humans join him in this rising movement. Then the whole of humanity together with all creation will take the giant step to new Life. "We shall all be changed." (1 Cor 15:55)

In the risen Jesus, the disciples saw this astonishing future clearly and as a certainty. The Second Coming, the general rising, became their vision of the world. There is no question that expectation of and longing for the all-inclusive coming of Christ was more central to the consciousness of the very early church than it is among most Christians today. For them, it was imminent. After all, it had been right before their eyes in Jesus Risen. Now, centuries later, we must say that they had the event right, but their timing was too optimistic. Even in the Book of Revelation dating from late in the first century, the author presents the Christ as saying, "Behold I make all things new." (Rev. 21:5) Then in the next chapter the Christ repeats three times, "Behold, I am coming soon." In response to this promise, we have the final words of the Bible, "Amen! Come, Lord Jesus!" The Aramaic form of these words is *Marana tha*, Come, Lord. It is no exaggeration to characterize the spirituality of the first Christians as Maranatha mysticism.

However, the early disciples were not a tight little group watching and waiting for the Coming, content to let the rest of the world go to perdition. This would be utterly contrary to their resurrection vision. The all-powerful dynamism of the Christ encounters impelled them as enlightened witnesses to proclaim the New Age to all peoples. I feel increasingly drawn to this spirituality. I am discovering more and more the enthusiasm essential to the Christ dynamic.

From my study of English poetry almost sixty years ago, the drastically mistaken words of Swinburne come to mind. "Thou hast conquered, O pale Galilean. The world has grown grey from thy breath." (Hymn to Proserpine, Goddess of death) The experience of millions is directly the opposite: "Thou hast conquered, alive Galilean. The world has grown radiant with thy breath."

Together with Jesus of Nazareth and all the great spiritual leaders of humanity we are, all of us, on the resplendent path to new life. We are always pilgrims.

Notes

Unless otherwise noted, all citations from the Holy Bible refer to the following edition:New Revised Standard Version Holy Bible: Catholic Edition. Oxford University Press, 2000.

Part 1

Introduction

1.   Walter Abbot, ed. *Notes of the Vatican*. New York: The American Press, 1966, p. 349.

2.   Ibid.

3.   Ibid. p. 116.

4.   Rabindranath Tagore. "Closed Path." in *Gitanjali (Song Offerings)*. London: MacMillan, 1913.

Chapter 1: Before Going Over

1.   St. Augustine. *The Confesssions*.

Chapter 2: Going Over

1.   Karl Rahner, S.J. *Nature and Grace*. New York, Sheed & Weed, 1964, p. 116.

2.   Ibid. p. 118

3.   Ibid. p. 135.

Chapter 3: Into Zen

1.   Beatrice Bruteau. *What We Can Learn From the East*. Crosswind/Herder & Herder, 1995.

Chapter 4: Dokusan

1.   Mumon. *Mumonkan: The Gateless Barrier*, Case #11. Translation . by Thomas J. Hand.

Chapter 5: Practice

1.   John Stevens. *The Marathon Monks of Mount Hiei*. Boston: Shambhala Press, 1988, pp. 72-73.

2.   Ibid, p. 106.

Chapter 6: Zazen

1.   Mumon. *Mumonkan: The Gateless Barrier*, Case #11. Translation by Thomas J. Hand.

2.   St. Augustine, *The Confesssions*.

3.   Quoted in Paul Reps. *Zen Flesh, Zen Bones*. Anchor Books, 1961.

4.   Quoted in Philip Kapleau. *The Three Pillars of Zen*. Garden City, New York: Anchor Books, Doubleday, 1980, pp. 171-172.

5.   Ken Wilbur. *A Brief History of Everything*. Boston: Shambhala, 1996, p. 217.

Chapter 7: Self-Discovery

1.   Kapleau, *The Three Pillars of Zen*, p. 157.

2.   Quoted in Marilyn Ferguson. *The Aquarian Conspiracy*. Los Angeles: J.P. Tarcher, Inc., 1980, pp. 30-31.

Chapter 8: The Empty-Full Self

1.   For the full account, see Kapleau, *The Three Pillars of Zen*, pp. 215-219.

2.   Philip Kapleau. *Zen, Merging of East and West*. New York: Anchor Books, Doubleday, 1980, p. 64.

3.   Kapleau, *The Three Pillars of Zen*, pp. 218-219.

Chapter 9: The Bodhisattva Path

1.   Shantediva; Stephen Batchelor, trans. *A Guide to the Bodhisattva's Way of Life*. Library of Tibetan Works and Archives, 1979, pp. 23-25.

Part 2

Chapter 11: A Massive Change

1.   Kevin O'Shea. *Person in Cosmos*. Bristol, Indiana, Wyndam Hill Press, 1995, pp. 149-150.

2.   Adam Richardson. *Creeds in the Making*. Philadelphia: Trinity Press International, 1935, p. 9.

3.   Quoted in Richard McBrien. *Catholicism*. Minneapolis: Winston Press, 1981, p. 1194.

Chapter 14: God Talk I

1.   Yamada Mumon. "Waga Kokoro no Henreki." In *Te Wo Awaseru*. Publishing data untraced at this writing.

2.   Kapleau, *The Three Pillars of Zen*, p. 174.

3.   Kapleau, *The Three Pillars of Zen*, p. 192.

4.   Exodus 3:13-14. The full text reads: "God replied, *'I AM WHO I AM'. Then he added,* 'This is what you shall tell the Israelites I AM sent me to you." Note how smoothly the text reads without the part I put in italics. It seems probable that the name I AM was not a Hebrew word, so the italic part was added when the Hebrew language developed and was used for the Bible.

Chapter 15: God Talk II

1.   Douglas A. Fox. *The Heart of Buddhist Wisdom*. Edwin Mellen Press, Lewiston, N.Y., 1985.

Chapter 16: God and Us

1.   Jones, Wainwright, and Yarnold, eds. *The Study of Spirituality*. New York: Oxford University Press, 1986, p. 313.

2.   Arthur Koestler. *The Ghost in the Machine*. Macmillan, New York, 1967.

3.   Swani Abhishiktananda. *Hindu Christian Meeting Point*. Bombay: Institute of Indian Culture, 1969, p. 107.

4.   Ibid. p. 109.

Chapter 17: The God Field
1.   Joe E. Brown. Laughter is a Wonderful Thing. New York: A.S.
Barnes & Co., 1956, p. 272.
2.   Ibid. p. 125
3.   Alfred North Whitehead. "Religion and Dogma." in *Religion in the Making*. King's Chapel, Boston, 1921.
4.   Richard McBrien, *Catholicism*, p. 60.

Chapter 18: Holonic Christology
1.   The concept of *interbeing* is central to the teachings of Vietnamese Zen monk Thich Naht Hahn. His religious community is named the Order of Interbeing.

Chapter 20: An Outmoded Soteriology
1.   Tim LaHaye and Jerry B. Jenkins. *Left Behind*. Wheaton, IL: Tyndale House Publishers, Inc., 1995, p. 201.
2.   Alan Richardson. *An Introduction to the Theology of the Testament*. New York: Harper & Row, 1958, p. 215.
3.   Ibid. p. 239.
4.   Tim LaHaye and Jerry B. Jenkins. *Left Behind*, p. 201.

Chapter 21: Saved by Christ
1.   John Donne. Meditation XVII. In *The Norton Anthology of English Literature*. New York: Norton & Co., Inc., 1968, pp. 527-528.
2.   The phrase "the hundredth monkey" is from Ken Keys's book of that name. (Vision Books, Coos Bay, OR, 1982), Lyall Watson, who first reported this event to the general public, did not present the story of these monkeys as scientific but rather as anecdotal. Regardless of what happened in Kyushu, I maintain that the basic principle of our interconnectedness through our common form field is valid.

Chapter 24: Committed to Christ Energy

1.   Raymond E Brown. *The Birth of the Messiah*. Garden City, N.Y.: Image Books, 1977, p. 23.

2.   John L. McKenzie, S.J. *Dictionary of the Bible*. New York: Bruce Publishing Company, 1965, p. 552b.

3.   Joseph Mary Plunkett. *Poems of Joseph Mary Plunkett*. AMS Press, 1978.

Chapter 25: Finding Christ in Nature

1.   Gerald Manley Hopkins. "Binsey Poplars." *The Poems of Gerald Manley Hopkins*. Humpfrey Milford, London, 1918.

Chapter 26: Finding the Archetype in People

1.   Alice Walker. *The Color Purple*. New York: Harcourt Brace Jovanovich, 1982, p. 176.

2.   Ibid. p. 178.

Chapter 27: Becoming Christ in the Mass

1.   Walter Abbot, *Notes of the Vatican*, p. 142.

2.   Ibid. p. 28.

3.   *The Rites of the Catholic Church*. New York: Pueblo Publishing, 1976, p. 3.

4.   Eugene Peterson. *The Message*. Colorado Springs, CO: Navpress. 1993, p. 240.

Chapter 29: Always a Pilgrim

1.   This quotation and those of Mechtild and Eckhart are quoted in Matthew Fox. *Original Blessing*. Santa Fe, NM: Bear Co., 1982, pp.88-89.